Children with Learning Disabilities

Children with Learning Disabilities

Social Functioning and Adjustment

Dabie Nabuzoka
Sheffield Hallam University

THE BRITISH
PSYCHOLOGICAL
SOCIETY

First published in 2000 by BPS Books (The British Psychological Society), St Andrews House, 48 Princess Road East, Leicester LE1 7DR, UK.

A catalogue record for this book is available from the British Library.

Library of Congress Cataloging-in-Publication Data on file.

ISBN 1 85433 326 7

Typeset by Book Production Services, London.
Printed in Great Britain by MPG Books Limited.

Contents

Preface

In recent years there has been an increased interest in the social and emotional adjustment of children with learning disabilities (LD) especially in integrated mainstream schools. There is some general agreement among researchers of social development that such children face problems in social relations and that the nature of such problems may be related to aspects of the presenting disability. This may have to do with how children with LD understand social situations and behave in those contexts, and also how other children and significant others perceive and relate to them. However, there are those who attribute such difficulties to underlying deficits that also explain difficulties in the academic domain, while others consider problems in social relations to represent a specific area of difficulty. This book particularly examines ways in which social understanding (social cognitive functioning) of children with LD may underpin the nature of their interaction with non-LD peers, and discusses ways in which this may be related to their social adjustment in school settings.

Although a number of books have been published about children with LD, few have addressed possible links between social understanding of these children and their social adjustment and adaptation in integrated settings such as mainstream schools. Various publications on children with LD have separately addressed the topics of social cognitive development, social perception and adjustment or adaptation. However, the bulk of this work has tended to be fragmented and is published in specialist or professional journals with varied levels of accessibility to many with interest in the social development of these children. The idea behind this book therefore, was to provide a synthesis of some of the work on social cognitive functioning of children with LD, and to examine how such functioning may account for social adjustment of these children. I have been involved in some of this work over the last decade or so since my earlier work on children with disabilities in Zambia. It is from such involvement that I got the impetus to compile the various research findings on the subject with a view to drawing theoretical and practical implications from them. There has also been a growing recognition, both from my own work with children with LD and also the literature, that social ecological factors are also important in the manifestation, if not the aetiology, of presenting difficulties of children with LD. I have therefore attempted to incorporate such considerations in this volume.

A number of people have contributed in various ways to the publication of this book and deserve a few words of thanks. My first thanks go to all those children with disabilities that I have worked with over the years. Much of my own work that is cited in this book was conducted with Professor Peter K. Smith of Goldsmiths College, University of London, while at Sheffield University. I have been privileged to work with Professor Smith on similar projects since then. Professor Robert Serpell of University of Maryland at Baltimore gave me the original guidance and inspiration to work with children with disabilities from way back in Zambia. His influence is greatly appreciated. Dr Janet Empson read various drafts of some chapters and provided useful comments. Dr Empson has been a valuable colleague at Sheffield Hallam University. Professor John Rønning of University of Tromsø has been a most valued professional colleague and personal friend also dating back to my early work in Zambia. Professor Rønning read and provided comments on some drafts of the book and greatly contributed to the work cited in a number of chapters. Many thanks also to Miss Tutsirai Nabuzoka who drafted Figure 7.1. A number of people at BPS Books have also been helpful, patient and supportive during the course of preparation and publication of this book: Jon Reed, former Senior Editor; Joyce Collins, Head of Publishing; and Rachel Gear, Editorial Assistant. I am grateful to all of them.

Finally, greatest thanks to my family who have had to endure my long hours of 'antisocial activities' with the computer during the course of writing this book: my wife Jennis, and daughters Tutsirai and Chikobwe. They have also provided some useful insights into important aspects of the social functioning and adjustment of children in the context of the school. Their patience and support is greatly appreciated.

Introduction

The term 'learning disability' is used variously to include (a) those individuals whose problems are characterized by difficulties in the academic domain (this being the dominant usage in the US, for example); and/or (b) those with intellectual disabilities characterized by a low intelligence quotient (this being the common usage in the UK). The children who are the subject of this book relate mostly to the former category but may also fall towards the more able end of the latter category. Various studies have indicated consistently that a large number of such children with learning disabilities (LD) not only have problems in the academic domain but also experience difficulties with significant people in their lives. The nature of these difficulties can best be studied in the school setting where children spend much of their time. In the last few decades, the policy in most countries – including the UK and the US – has been to integrate children with LD into mainstream schools, where they are likely to come into regular contact with peers without learning disabilities.

In the school setting, peer relations are important because they play a significant role in social and emotional development. However, research indicates that many children with LD are more likely to experience problems with peer relations in integrated school settings. In such an environment, children with LD experience 'negative' social relationships with peers and tend to be regarded less positively by teachers. These children also report more dissatisfaction and anxiety about their peer relations. One explanation for this is that children with LD are impaired in their perception and understanding of social events, and that this accounts for the nature and quality of their overall social functioning and adjustment (Spafford and Grosser, 1993). For example, they may misperceive situations owing to difficulties in detecting and understanding important person and contextual cues. Such diminished sensitivity to subtle social cues can lead to inappropriate responses to overtures of others, and frequent displays of inappropriate responses can in turn result in the child being less well regarded by peers or significant others, and having 'negative' experiences. This explanation has led many researchers to focus on the relationship between cognitive and behavioural aspects of the social functioning of these children (Maheady and Sainato, 1986; Kravetz *et al.*, 1999; Spafford and Grosser, 1993).

There is thus a hypothesized relationship between social understanding (social cognition), behavioural attributes (dispositions), and the quality of social relations (social adjustment) of children with LD. According to this view, the nature and quality of social relations experienced by the child is said to originate from the individual child's social cognitive functioning such that problems in social relations may ultimately be linked to social cognitive deficits. Such a theoretical model has been influential among researchers of social development and offers a possible explanation for the social problems that children with LD may experience. The model is illustrated and elaborated further in Chapter 1. Theoretically, adequate social cognitive skills are necessary prerequisites for successful social interaction, as one's appraisal and understanding of situations may have a bearing on behaviour, which in turn could account for others' appraisal of the individual.

This book examines the theoretical and empirical bases for the foregoing model. Various aspects of the domains involved in the model and the relationships between them are discussed.

First, in Chapter 1, a number of issues relating to social functioning and adjustment of children with LD are introduced. One issue relates to the terminology used to define the population of concern, and to explain the nature of their difficulties. It is suggested that the social dimension to their problems can best be understood by examining the relationship between aspects of functioning and the general construct of 'social competence'. A framework is provided within which such problems are considered to have a basis in social cognitive functioning. Dimensions of the model linking social cognitive functioning and quality of social relations experienced by an individual are outlined. Approaches to studies of children with and without learning disabilities, in which findings reflect such links in the social cognitive model, are discussed briefly to set the scene for subsequent chapters.

Although the model identifies an individual's social adjustment as being related directly to his or her social cognitive and behavioural functioning, it is recognized that such adjustment may be a function *also* of the interaction of variables intrinsic to the child, as well as to contextual variables. Behavioural and social adjustment measures as considered in this book have a strong social ecological component, both because they depend on other people as referents, and because they occur in given contexts. They may thus be greatly influenced by the perspectives of those with whom the children interact and the context to which the assessments refer. Social ecological factors are therefore recognized as moderating variables.

Chapter 2 examines the role of the school environment in the social cognitive development of children with LD. A major concern has been to determine what promotes optimal development: the integrated mainstream setting or the segregated special school. The relative effects of each of these settings on the social functioning and adjustment of children with LD are examined and discussed in the context of the role of social ecological factors in the social development of children generally, and of children with LD in particular.

There are, however, aspects of social functioning that reflect skills intrinsic to individual children, and social perception is one such aspect. Chapter 3 considers the abilities of children with LD in this domain. An individual's perceptions of social cues and events are aspects of cognition that influence social behaviour. Of concern is whether any differences between children with LD and non-LD peers are developmental in nature, and whether they reflect social perceptual deficits for children with LD. Specifically, do these differences reflect quantitative or qualitative differences in the functioning of children with LD; and what significance do they have for intervention approaches aimed at children with LD?

In this respect, some emphasis has been placed on establishing the mechanisms by which social perceptual skills may be linked to behavioural outcomes. Social perceptual skills have sometimes been taken to include abilities such as social perspective taking and empathic skills. Of significant interest in studies has been the hypothesis that children with LD have problems in interpersonal interaction which may be due to the same complex phenomena that produce their learning problems (Spafford and Grosser, 1993).

Some descriptions of characteristics of children with LD related to social perception and associated social problems have identified subtypes of disabilities. Over the last decade or so, there has been increasing interest in the use of subtyping techniques for research into and treatment of LD, and Little (1993) has provided a useful review. Rourke (1989), for example, posited two primary types: the 'non-verbal LD syndrome' and the 'verbal (phonological) LD syndrome'. In this schema, those with non-verbal LD are said to have social problem-solving deficits and difficulties with identifying non-verbal communications, resulting in poor overall social adaptation; whereas those with verbal LD may not have these same problems. While some studies have sought to clarify the relative significance of verbal and non-verbal LD on measures of social functioning (see Little, 1993), many of the studies reviewed in this book do not make such a distinction specifically. However, the relationship between problems in interpersonal interactions of children with LD and problems in verbal and non-verbal communications is discussed at length.

A more mechanistic view of social cognitive functioning of children with LD is discussed in Chapter 4. Social cognition is presented as involving various processes concerned with how one understands social situations, from perception of social cues to enactment of responses. Social cognitive functioning in the context of interpersonal interaction is considered to involve various levels of information processing. Children with LD are compared with non-LD peers on these aspects of social cognitive abilities, which are then related to behavioural attributes and the social adjustment of the children. The specific ways in which deficits in this area might account for the social adjustment problems of children with LD are examined and discussed. It is considered, in terms of social information processing, that problems can arise through impairment at any of the stages of interpretation of social cues, accessing of an appropriate response, or even the enactment of an appropriate response. Considering such functioning in the context of interpersonal interaction and social problem-solving has implications for the design of intervention programmes for children with LD.

Chapter 5 discusses the relationship between social behaviour and adjustment in the light of empirical studies on sociometric status and behaviour. Research has involved various measures, including peer nominations and ratings, teacher ratings, and direct observation of behaviour. Children with LD have typically been compared with non-LD children on these measures. The usefulness of obtaining measures of both behavioural attributes and social adjustment is that a relationship can be determined between social skills and their outcomes. However, the nature of this relationship may vary depending on the specific population being considered. The recognition of LD, in particular, may influence the perception of some behavioural attributes in ways that are different for non-LD peers. It is with such considerations that the significance of empirical findings on the relationship between social behaviour and adjustment of children with LD is discussed.

Chapter 6 provides an overview and synthesis of some findings linking various aspects of social cognition, behaviour and social adjustment of children with LD. The chapter presents data that provide some empirical evidence for linkages between the domains of social functioning and adjustment. An evaluation is made of the social cognitive deficit model of social adjustment problems. On the basis of the data presented, questions are addressed relating to the particular ways in which cognitive abilities are implicated in the behavioural characteristics of children with LD; and whether such characteristics represent social skills of these children that can be said to determine their level of social adjustment.

Chapter 7 discusses a number of issues. First, theoretical and conceptual difficulties inherent in much of the work on characteristics and modes of functioning of children with LD are outlined and discussed. Methodological problems that make it difficult to judge the relevance and usefulness of much of the research in this area are then addressed.

A specific concern is with applied research, which is important in the development and refinement of effective strategies to meet the needs of children with LD. It involves evaluation of the impact of service design and provision, and of the design and efficacy of intervention approaches aimed at individual children. An example of a service design for integration into mainstream schools is discussed.

Second, with regard to individual intervention strategies, a number of approaches have been tried with varying degrees of success. Some of these intervention approaches are outlined and discussed to illustrate central concerns. Finally, some space is devoted to discussing the necessity of integrating cognitive and social ecological research for a better understanding of the social problems that may be faced by children with learning disabilities.

Chapter 1

Social functioning and adjustment

This chapter introduces various issues relating to social functioning and adjustment of children with learning disabilities (LD). The terminology used to define the population of concern, and to explain the nature of their difficulties, is considered first. The social dimension to problems faced by these children is then considered by discussing the relationship between aspects of general functioning and the construct of 'social competence'. A framework is provided within which such problems are considered to be related to social cognition. Finally, the chapter discusses a theoretical model linking social cognitive functioning and the quality of social relations experienced by an individual, this being one explanation for the social problems that may be experienced by children with LD. Approaches to studies of children with or without LD, whose findings reflect such links, are discussed briefly to set the scene for subsequent chapters. As a running theme of the conceptual framework of this and subsequent chapters, the interactive nature of variables intrinsic to a child and contextual variables is emphasized.

Terminology and classification

The term 'learning disabilities' has acquired slightly different meanings in different parts of the world, notably as used in North America compared with Britain. It is of relatively recent origin as a category of special education. In the US, the term can be traced back to Samuel Kirk who proposed it at a meeting of parents in New York City in 1963. It had been used for the first time a year earlier in the first edition of his textbook *Educating Exceptional Children* (Kirk, 1962). Kirk (1963) proposed that the term should be used to denote the difficulties some children have in school-related basic skill areas (e.g. speech and language, reading, spelling, writing, maths). He emphasized the need to forego speculation about the causes of learning failure, and rather to focus on identifying and treating the learning problems themselves. There then followed a number of alternative definitions of LD to reflect an increasing awareness of the plight of 'disabled learners' and of the need to identify and treat their problems (Hallahan and Kauffman, 1976). However, the tendency within the education profession has been to retain a broader definition of learning disabilities, this being consistent with the proposal by Hallahan and Kauffman (1977) that a child with a learning disability is simply one who is not achieving his or her full potential. Such a child may have any intelligence level, may have a learning problem for any number of reasons (some perceptual and some not), and may or may not have emotional problems.

One of the key components in the definitions currently in use is a discrepancy between a child's aptitude and his or her achievement. In most cases, however, underachievement has tended to be the main basis of classification to LD status by educational or school committees (MacMillan *et al.*, 1998).

In Britain, 'people with learning disabilities' refers to the broader category of people with intellectual disabilities, including those who in the US and elsewhere are referred to as 'mentally retarded'. The latter term is not generally in common usage in Britain except in the context of some clinical discourse and journals. The current British definition and classification of children experiencing difficulties in the academic domain was influenced by the Warnock Report of 1978. Until then, such children were classified into various separate categories that included physical, emotional and intellectual difficulties (Pritchard, 1963). The Warnock Report recommended that the term 'children with learning difficulties' be used *for all children requiring special educational provision*, and that such learning difficulties might be described as 'mild', 'moderate' or 'severe'. Children with particular difficulties only, such as with reading, may be described as having a 'specific learning difficulty'. This classification represented a move away from using several categorical *labels*, towards statements of educational *needs* based on a detailed profile following an individual assessment.

These, then, are functional classifications based essentially on curricular requirements. They place more emphasis on what the child may require and less on the presenting limitations of the child. However, as pointed out by Dockrell and McShane (1993), identification of an appropriate curriculum for the child requires an understanding of the nature of the child's problems. An understanding of the child's cognitive abilities is therefore necessary when considering learning difficulties. Categorization solely on the basis of educational needs as suggested by the Warnock Report also tends to be too inclusive of children whose difficulties might be sensory, physical, emotional, or due to what has been referred to as 'intellectual disability' or 'mental handicap' (retardation). These difficulties represent different social experiences for the children affected and, when the concern is mainly with social functioning, such differences may not be reflected in a classification of special educational needs.

In this book the term 'learning disability' is generally used in a sense similar to that adopted in the US (i.e. difficulties in the academic domain). However, also included are children who, in the British sense, may be described as having learning difficulties arising from a mild intellectual disability (said to have 'mild mental retardation' in the US). This group of children includes those with Full Scale IQ (intelligence quotient) scores within one standard deviation below or above 100. These children are in most cases characterized by a discrepancy between aptitude and achievement but may be without any other apparent physical, sensory or emotional problems that could have a significant impact on their social functioning. They are those whose impairment is not such that education out of the mainstream is considered necessary. Because they tend to be integrated into mainstream schools, their social cognitive functioning has implications for their overall adjustment in these settings when compared with peers without learning disabilities (non-LD). Such functioning also reflects to a large extent an interaction between the variables that are intrinsic to the child and contextual variables. In this respect, some social ecological factors pertaining to the functioning of children with LD also require consideration.

Learning disability, social competence and adjustment

Learning disability and social competence

Although the term 'learning disabilities' may suggest difficulties primarily in the academic domain, problems are not confined to that area alone (Pearl *et al.*, 1986). Evidence suggests that people with LD encounter problems in their social relationships as well (Bender and Smith, 1990; Kavale and Forness, 1996; Pearl *et al.*, 1986). As pointed out by Bryan and Bryan (1978), the factors that first set children with this 'label' apart from their classmates, thus setting in motion the referral and diagnostic process, tend to be problems in social adjustment rather than just academic underachievement. However, although descriptions of individuals with LD have included some social characteristics, it is only relatively recently that attention has been paid during assessment and intervention to social behaviours, especially peer-related interactions. Until recently, the major concern was academic difficulties and how to address them. A child's general perceptual and cognitive development was the main factor related to academic success or failure. In the last few decades, however, efforts have been made to relate perceptual and cognitive development of children also to social functioning and social competence (Dodge, 1986; Shantz, 1975, 1983). Such a relationship has also been used to explain the nature and quality of social relations experienced by children with LD (Spafford and Grosser, 1993; Stiliadis and Wiener, 1989).

An important approach to studying the social relations of children with LD has been to evaluate them in terms of the general construct of 'social competence'. Various attempts have been made to specify what constitutes social competence as generally applied to individuals (e.g. Dodge *et al.*, 1986; McFall, 1982). Terms such as 'social adequacy', 'social adjustment', 'social effectiveness' and 'social success' have been taken to refer to social competence without any generally accepted definition. This is partly because social competence does not refer to any specific set of capacities, but rather is an underlying construct reflecting a common element among several different sets of capacities. There has, however, been some agreement on two primary indices: patterns of social behaviour, and judgements by other individuals (Furman, 1984; Spence, 1991). Thus, one can refer to patterns of behaviour as reflecting competence in interpersonal interaction if, as a result, the person is considered positively by others such as peers. In this sense, social competence has been associated with success in interpersonal relations.

It has been suggested that social competence in this sense is an evaluative term as it reflects an individual's judgement about the quality of another person's performance on a given social task (McFall, 1982). This has to be distinguished from social skills that refer to 'the specific overt and cognitive behaviours required in order to produce positive outcomes from interactions with others' (Spence, 1991, p. 149). A judgement about the social competence of a child therefore reflects the outcome or consequences of that child's behaviour in terms of evaluation by others.

Social competence can thus be considered as a construct embodying discrete elements of social skills, the acquisition of which is important for one's success in social relations (Gresham and Elliot, 1987). These skills can include the ability to detect and interpret important contextual and person cues – verbal as well as non-verbal – and the ability to relate and respond appropriately to other people's overtures. In this manner, models of social skills emphasize the cognitive as well as the overt behavioural components of responding to social situations (Dodge, 1986; McFall, 1982; Yeates and Selman, 1989). The socially competent individual experiences more 'positive' social relations as a result.

One way of operationalizing the 'quality' of children's social relations is to say that it refers to the qualitatively various sociometric positions existing in a group of children (Cillessen, 1991). The position of a child in these group relations is his or her *sociometric status*. Such group relations are referred to in terms of general acceptance or rejection. In this sense, for example, children experiencing 'positive' social relations will be popular among peers and generally liked by others. Those experiencing 'negative' relations may be rejected or neglected by peers and thus likely to experience loneliness. These group relations are distinguished from *dyadic relations* that may be referred to in terms of friendship and animosity, and may themselves be considered to contribute to the quality of social relations (Ladd, 1989; Hartup, 1989).

In this book, *the quality of social relations of children with LD refers to how others relate to the child and the responses of that child*. It is conceived as an outcome of others' evaluation of a given child. Because such relations define the social experiences of the child, they can be said to constitute the overall social adjustment of that particular individual. Social adjustment in this respect may be considered to be a consequence of the child's social skills and the resultant evaluation of the child by other people. It includes both the responses of other people (e.g. liked most and hence popular, or liked least and thus rejected/neglected), and the subjective experiences of the child (e.g. feelings of anxiety, loneliness or satisfaction about relations with others). Such a conceptualization of children's social functioning is depicted in Figure 1.1.

Learning disability and social adjustment

There has been consistent evidence that many children with LD experience 'negative' social relationships with significant people in their lives and even with strangers (Bickett and Milich, 1990; Gresham and Reschly, 1986). They are less well regarded by parents (Chapman and Boersma, 1979; McLoughlin *et al.*, 1987), by teachers (Cardell and Parmar, 1988; Garrett and Crump, 1980; Merrell, 1991), by other adult observers or strangers (Bryan and Perlmutter, 1979; Perlmutter and Bryan, 1984) and by peers (Nabuzoka and Smith, 1993; Stone and LaGreca, 1990; Swanson and Malone, 1992; Tur-Kaspa *et al.*, 1999). Children with LD also report more dissatisfaction and anxiety about their peer relations than do other children (Taylor *et al.*, 1987; Tur-Kaspa *et al.*, 1999). As children with LD are more likely to be regarded negatively by others and thus have 'negative experiences',

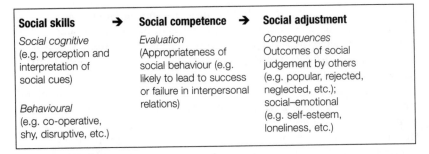

Figure 1.1 *Children's social functioning: distinguishing social skills, social competence and social adjustment*

the quality of their social relations can be said to be relatively poor.

According to the social skills model of adjustment, children with LD can be considered to experience relatively more social adjustment problems as a consequence of the children's social skills limitations or deficits and others' responses to them (Spafford and Grosser, 1993; Stiliadis and Wiener, 1993). The social skills model of adjustment has proved to be valuable, leading to considerable progress in identifying abilities associated with socially competent performance and in developing intervention programmes for fostering them (Chalmers and Townsend, 1990; Spence, 1985, 1991). For children with LD, identifying the skills that might need fostering needs to be an ongoing and integral part of the intervention process.

In this book, the social adjustment of children with LD, especially with regard to the quality of peer relations, is examined in relation to the acquisition or possession of those abilities associated with social competence. A cognitive frame of reference is taken by examining how social cognitive abilities may be related to other aspects of social functioning and also the social adjustment of such children.

The conceptual framework

Social context

Social behaviours of children with LD (and hence the social skills manifested) tend to be situation-specific. Whilst one can talk of *general* behavioural predisposition, social functioning of children with LD will, for conceptual clarity, be discussed mainly – though not exclusively – in the context of the school setting. Because a significant portion of children's time is spent in school, this is an ideal environment in which to study social functioning and adjustment. Of particular interest are relationships with peers, as these are considered to influence social and emotional development (Asher and Parker, 1989).

The extent to which the school setting may stimulate the social cognitive development of children with LD is largely mediated by its social ecology. In most cases the design of the social environment in schools is a policy issue. In Great Britain, for example, Education Acts in 1981 made provision for integration of children with special needs (including LD) into mainstream schools in England and Wales, and also in Scotland (see Morris *et al.*, 1995). Various models of provision have since been implemented. These range from partial integration, whereby a special unit is set up in a mainstream school, to full integration under which children with LD attend the same classes as their non-LD peers. From a social learning theory perspective, such contexts offer different levels of opportunities for children with LD to acquire 'appropriate' social skills through observation of others. At the level of policy formulation and its implementation, provision for children with LD can be said to reflect society's conceptualization of presenting problems (Acton, 1982).

According to Clements (1987), the most common response to individuals with disabilities has been to regard them as a homogeneous population, encouraging the formation of general social models to 'mediate the interpretation of presenting phenomena and provide some kind of philosophical framework to guide and rationalise society's response' (p. 2). These models have included sociological, medical and educational types, each of which has been predominant at various times in history. For example, one vein of the sociological model that grew up in the 1960s regarded people with intellectual disability as a deprived minority group for whom service provision and resource allocation were a human right to which they needed a fair share. Medical models regard intellectual disability as another illness needing professional treatment in a health context. Educational models, on the other hand, view intellectual disability from the functional perspective of learning and emphasize the need for services to be provided within an educational context, rather than a health one.

In recent years a characteristic shift in dominant models has involved the medical model being replaced by an educational model linked to a human rights and sociological approach. This has resulted in some rapid moves towards increased care and integration, and increased control of services by education and social welfare agencies rather than health agencies (cf. DHSS, 1980; Clements, 1987). The predominant social model has, to some extent, influenced the psychology of disability – exemplified in the shifting of educational policy in the UK, the US and other parts of the world towards integrating children with disabilities into the ordinary classroom (or at least the ordinary school). It has been argued, by analysts such as Stobart (1986), that though the outcomes of such policies have been couched in psychological terminology, the justification for integration has been based on appeals for social justice (cf. Fish Report, 1985) rather than on specific psychological or even educational grounds. According to Stobart, 'psychological theories have been conscripted to handle the psychological implications of this policy, which are usually construed as social, rather than academic benefits' (p. 1). Such a rationale for psychological enquiry is nonetheless relevant as far as the social functioning of children with LD is concerned.

Theoretical framework

A concern of many researchers is to determine the nature of developmental problems faced by children with LD. In the context of integrated schools, an important issue to address is the problems that might arise from the specific requirements for children with LD to function amongst more cognitively able peers. Explaining these problems requires a conceptual framework. Clements (1987), for example, identifies two major psychological theories that have been proposed to explain intellectual disability and which are seen as relevant for children with LD. One of these, the deviancy theory, considers those with intellectual disability to have one or more mental processes that are different from those in the normal population, and thus underlie low performance in various tasks. It emphasizes differences rather than commonalties between those affected and other members of society. The other theory is the developmental delay theory, which proposes that people with intellectual disability have the same mental processes as other people and go through the same stages of development as others – but at a slower rate.

These theoretical frameworks guide service delivery policies in different ways. Deviancy theory is in support of the sociological model that encouraged enforced segregation (to be distinguished from the human rights one), and in support of the medical model. Developmental delay theory, on the other hand, seems to be in tune with a sociological human rights model and, in so far as knowledge of developmental processes is regarded as relevant to education, with the education models.

A central question of concern is whether children with LD are delayed in their development or whether they have a different developmental *pattern*. Dockrell and McShane (1993) suggest that because children with general LD display a slower rate of learning and reach a lower ceiling, this indicates some limits on the extent of cognitive development, and that upper limits on performance exist. They pose the question as to whether the learning process of children with LD is best explained by a model which invokes the same principles and mechanisms of development that apply to other children, or whether it is necessary to invoke specific differences over and above the slower rate and lower ceiling.

Two main foci of studies have been identified addressing the question of developmental difference versus delay:

- establishing the extent to which children with general LD follow a similar sequence of development to typically developing children;
- establishing the extent to which performance differences on cognitive tasks can be explained by underlying processing differences (Dockrell and McShane, 1993).

Studies investigating the similar-sequence hypothesis consider children's progress through stages, such as the Piagetian stages of cognitive development. Research support for the similar-sequence hypothesis both across large stages and within the substages is considered important. For example, research on typically developing children has indicated some sequential order of developmental levels in interpersonal understanding (Selman, 1980; Gurucharri and Selman, 1982). Similar research on social perception of children with LD has sought to identify some developmental progression similar to that of non-LD children (Jackson *et al.*, 1987; Nabuzoka and Smith, 1995; see Chapter 3). The concern of such research is predominantly with what stages the child has mastered and in what order.

The other perspective is to consider how the child's cognitive system processes information. A suggestion is that children with LD process information in a manner different from that of typically developing children and that this accounts for difficulties they may experience across a wide range of tasks. According to this perspective, learning disabilities are seen in terms of cognitive processes and structures that may be absent or inefficient, thereby leading to poor performance across tasks. However, Dockrell and McShane (1993) argue that processing difficulties should not necessarily imply cognitive differences. They suggest that it might be more useful to consider how the cognitive system of children with LD might function differently to account for slower rates of development. One could also add that a major consideration should be the fact that cognition in the social domain differs significantly from non-social cognition (Clements, 1987).

The perspective focusing on the structure and functioning of cognitive processes of children with LD represents what has been termed the 'primary cause hypothesis'. This attributes social difficulties of children with LD to the same processes that produce learning dysfunction. The 'secondary cause hypothesis', on the other hand, explains difficulties of children with LD as resulting from the consequences of interpersonal processes such as low self-esteem and feelings of inferiority arising from repeated school failure (Vogel and Forness, 1992). The latter perspective views social and behavioural difficulties of children with LD as secondary to their cognitive problems. The former perspective thus emphasizes factors intrinsic to the child, while the latter includes a consideration of the role of social ecological factors.

Consideration of the role of social ecological factors is consistent with the view of a number of researchers who see the quality of children's peer relations as being related reciprocally to the development of social competence (Asher and Parker, 1989; Cillessen, 1991; Gresham and Elliot, 1989). For example, Gresham and Elliot pointed out that children with LD who achieve less peer acceptance than their peers may have fewer opportunities to engage in social interactions and to accumulate the social experience for interpersonal understanding. Such children would have less developed social skills and as a result would be considered less socially competent, thus being likely to be less accepted and to experience social experiences of rejection or neglect. According to this view, the suggestion that deficient interpersonal understanding or social cognition mediates the social and behavioural problems of children with LD is consistent with both the primary and secondary cause hypotheses. This is discussed further in Chapter 7.

In all, examination of the social functioning of children with LD, motivated by the desire to identify causes of social maladjustment, entails identifying skills that such children possess and determining whether, and how, they apply them in social contexts. Such skills may be in the cognitive domain, relating to social knowledge and understanding; or the skills may be behavioural, relating to characteristic ways of behaving towards others. These domains are not independent, and it has been argued that such skills constitute a part of the general construct of 'social competence'. This competence may be manifested in interpersonal interaction that may best be considered as involving a series of social tasks (Goldfried and d'Zurilla, 1969). For example, a child faced with provocation by a peer has the social task of how best to respond; or another child in a rough-and-tumble has to decide whether a peer is seriously aggressive or simply play-fighting, and then respond accordingly. Both these situations have a cognitive dimension (understanding of the requirements of the situation) and a behavioural one (how best to respond within one's repertoire). Children with LD have been found to perform worse than their peers on such social problem-solving tasks, thus apparently rendering support to the primary deficit hypothesis (Nabuzoka and Smith, 1999; Smith, 1986).

Another possibility to consider, however, is that children with LD may acquire social skills more slowly – such that they are unable to build up requisite age-appropriate knowledge and strategies to perform social tasks successfully. Such deficiencies in execution may appear to reflect a different cognitive structuring, and it has been suggested that they should be considered as defining characteristics of learning disabilities (McConaughy and Ritter, 1986). However, while a child with difficulties in identifying appropriate strategies to use in problem-solving situations may appear to have a cognitive system functioning differently, the portrayed behaviour may simply reflect an inappropriate basis for responding. For example, children with LD have been found also to be less proactive and more passive in social tasks. Their poor performance may therefore arise from this predisposition, rather than reflect different cognitive structures *per se* (Bryan *et al.*, 1981a; 1981b; Dockrell and McShane, 1993).

It is also important to distinguish social skill *deficits* from skill *inhibition*. A social cognitive frame of analysis is concerned with the primary cause of behaviour as solely intrinsic to the child. In this case, inappropriate or non-responsive behaviour may be attributable to social cognitive deficits. However, an apparent lack of appropriate skills may be a result of cognitive processes such as low self-esteem and feelings of inferiority as a result of repeated failure. These are likely to be outcomes of interpersonal processes related to the attitudes and responses of others. These processes have a social ecological dimension related to one's previous experiences in similar situations. A child may, for example, have some anxiety, anger or depression as a result of unsatisfying peer relations.

The nature of social cognitive factors at play, and the interaction of such factors with behavioural dispositions and social factors are therefore important elements to consider. When analysing the particular ways in which these variables contribute to social adjustment of children with LD, the presence or absence of LD is an independent variable, and social cognition is a mediating variable between this and behaviour and, through the latter, social adjustment.

The social cognitive basis of adjustment

Social skill models of adjustment generally agree that a series of cognitive problem-solving steps determines a child's behavioural response in a social situation (Spence, 1987, 1991; Dodge, 1986).

The first step is social perception in which one receives and interprets social information. This information concerns the context of the situation and the social cues elicited by others with whom one is interacting. At this stage one should determine the demands, requirements and expectations of the task at hand. Knowledge of social rules and meaning of social information plays an important role in determining accurate social perception.

Having identified the nature of the social task, the child's next step is to generate a range of alternative responses or solutions. The response alternatives are then evaluated for their likely consequences and the child is required to select a response that is most likely to lead to a 'positive' outcome. The response selected should be within the behavioural repertoire of the child. After selecting an appropriate response strategy, the child must be able to perform the action successfully.

The final stage of social information processing is said to involve monitoring of one's own performance and the reaction of other people to the response strategy selected. This step is essentially an evaluation of outcomes, and in many respects this process reflects a social perception step requiring the skills of attention, correct interpretation and social knowledge (Spence, 1991).

Children may have difficulties with any of the stages of information processing, with consequences for their social relations. For example, difficulties in the area of social perception would arise for children with difficulties in receiving social information (due, for example, to

Figure 1.2 *A social cognitive model of adjustment*

sensory impairment or attention deficits), or for children with limited social knowledge. There may also be difficulties if the child has a limited range of options that can be generated as solutions to a social problem. Furthermore, difficulties can arise if the child cannot predict the consequences of various response choices.

For children with LD, it has been suggested that problems may arise from their behaviour being inappropriate and the tone of their behaviour being inconsistent (Pearl *et al.*, 1986). A social cognitive explanation is that, even though the child may intend to behave appropriately, he or she may fail to do so through misunderstanding the situation. This may be due to difficulty in detecting or processing important information from person and contextual cues. This can frequently lead to inappropriate responses to overtures of others, which in turn results in the child being less well regarded by peers or significant others and being a recipient of 'negative' experiences.

The argument that impairment in social perception and understanding of children with LD accounts for their social adjustment problems has been referred to as the 'social cognitive deficit hypothesis' (Nabuzoka, 1999). This model or hypothesis emphasizes the mediating role of social cognitive functioning between the presence and absence of LD on the one hand, and the nature of social adjustment on the other. Figure 1.2 shows a model of the hypothesized relationship between social cognition (including social perception), social behaviour, and general social adjustment.

This model can be considered to represent the various stages in the process of social adaptation and adjustment of children with LD. According to the model, the basis of an individual's social adjustment is social cognitive functioning or social understanding. It is suggested that skills in this domain are reflected in the individual's behaviour, which forms the basis on which others make judgements and ultimately base their treatment of that individual (Dodge, 1986). A child's social experiences, his or her peer relations, are thus a reflection of others' responses to the child's dispositions, which are in turn determined by his or her social cognitive functioning.

Later chapters examine the extent to which research supports such a social cognitive model of social adjustment of children with LD. For example, the model in Figure 1.2 may be too unilinear, thus ignoring the reciprocal nature of relations between an individual's functional domains. However, while an acknowledgement should be made regarding the reciprocal nature of some of the issues explored, greater emphasis is on examining the extent to which findings from various studies support such a unilinear model. The rationale for specific areas of focus, and the general trends of research findings on each relevant area, are first introduced briefly in the sections below.

Social perception

Social perception is defined as the ability to interpret and label social cues such as posture, gestures, facial expression and tone of voice (Spence, 1985, 1991), including also contextual cues. An individual's social perceptual skills therefore constitute an important aspect of his or her overall ability to understand a social environment.

Some studies have focused on comparing the performance of children with and without LD on tasks developed to measure the ability to perceive and interpret emotions (Axelrod, 1982; Bryan, 1977; Holder and Kirkpatrick, 1991; Nabuzoka and Smith, 1995; Sprouse *et al.*, 1998; Wiig and Harris, 1974). Children with LD often perform relatively poorly on such tasks, and this has been taken to indicate that they are impaired in their ability to perceive social cues. Some analysts have thus suggested that inadequate social perception be considered one of the identifying characteristics of many children with LD (McConaughy and Ritter, 1986; Myklebust, 1975), specifically those with non-verbal LD (Johnson and Myklebust, 1967; Rourke, 1989).

Other studies have been conducted on social perspective-taking. These have found difficulties for children with LD in skills involving empathy (Bachara, 1976), role-taking (Dickstein and Warren, 1980) and making social inferences (Bruno, 1981). Social perception abilities are, however, not considered as being synonymous with social perspective-taking and empathic skills. (The latter has been defined as the extent to which an individual is able to set aside privileged or personal knowledge and emotions and adopt the perspective of another person; see Chalmers and Townsend, 1990.) Such abilities may be related to social perception, but they also reflect cognitive abilities that influence the spectrum of social cognitive skills, including social problem-solving skills (Spence, 1991; Yeates and Selman, 1989). In this book, a distinction is made between social perception skills involving such abilities as recognition of emotions, on the one hand, and social perspective-taking and empathic skills on the other. The latter two abilities can be considered in the context of social problem-solving skills as reflected in social information processing.

Social information processing

The processing of social information by a child has generally been considered in terms of social problem-solving skills. This includes extracting meaning from a wide range of cues and sources of information, such as the nature of the social situation, speech, body postures and facial expressions of others. It also involves analysis of any information from other people concerning their thoughts and feelings; using the analysis to make inferences and generate expectations about their inner state and overt behaviour; and using such inferences and expectations to guide one's behaviour in the situation at hand. Children with problems in processing social information are likely to have difficulty in understanding their social world and may thus function less effectively in social interactions. However, while a number of studies have examined the social information processing skills of non-LD children, there have been very few studies directly investigating similar abilities in children with LD. The relevant studies – for example, Nabuzoka (1993) and Gomez and Hazeldine (1996) – were based on the social information processing model proposed by Dodge (1986, Dodge *et al.*, 1986).

According to Dodge's model, a child's behavioural response in a social situation follows a set of sequential information processing steps. These include:

- encoding the social cues from the environment (step 1);
- forming a mental representation and interpretation of those cues (step 2);
- searching for a possible behavioural response (step 3);
- deciding on a response from those generated (step 4);
- enacting the selected response (step 5).

Deficiencies in processing, such as inaccurate interpretation of a peer's intent, or biased responses, would lead to socially inappropriate or problem behaviour. Thus, poor social information processing has been linked to poor peer relationships and other indices of maladjustment (Dodge and Frame, 1982; Murphy *et al.*, 1992; Quiggle *et al.*, 1992; for a review, see Crick and Dodge, 1994).

Research generally indicates that children with LD may have less developed social cognitive skills relating to perception (Holder and Kirkpatrick, 1991; Nabuzoka and Smith, 1995) and to the analysis or processing of social information (Gomez and Hazeldine, 1996; Nabuzoka, 1993; Nabuzoka and Smith, 1999). According to the social skills model of adjustment, adequate social cognitive skills are necessary prerequisites for successful social interaction. This is because an individual's appraisal and understanding of situations may have a bearing on his or her behaviour in any context, which in turn can account for others' appraisal of the individual (Dodge *et al.*, 1986). An important task for researchers, therefore, is to establish an empirical relationship between social cognitive functioning and social adjustment as mediated by behaviour of children with LD. Establishing such a relationship first entails a documentation of the effects of the presence or absence of LD on the social behaviour of children, as well as the particular ways in which such behaviour may reflect social cognitive functioning (see Kravetz *et al.*, 1999).

Social behaviour

Various methods are used to assess children's behaviour, including teacher and parent ratings, direct observation of interactions, self-reports, and peer nominations (Williams and Gilmour, 1994). A substantial number of studies have compared the behaviour of children with LD with that of non-LD children. A proportion have sought to establish a link between social cognitive functioning and behaviour of children with LD, and between the children's behaviour and their social relations as reflected in measures of acceptance or sociometric status. Findings from these studies have implications for our understanding of the social cognitive basis of social functioning and adjustment.

A number of studies have suggested that children with LD often may *not* be withdrawn or isolated in their interactions with others – they have been observed to participate in interactions with other children as much as non-LD children (Pearl *et al.*, 1986; Roberts *et al.*, 1991). It is therefore more useful to consider the *nature* and *quality* of such interactions. There are suggestions, for example, that the tone of the behaviour of children with LD may differ from that typical of others, such that they may not be appropriately responsive to other people's overtures (Mathinos, 1991; Speckman, 1981). Inappropriate behaviour in this sense may be responsible for difficulties experienced in social relations as evidenced by the low regard with which children with LD are held (Gresham and Reschly, 1986). According to a social skill model of adjustment, such behaviour may be a result of social misperception and impaired communication skills (Spafford and Grosser, 1993). In this way social cognitive factors would be implicated in the social functioning (behaviour) and adjustment of children with LD.

Confirmation of the pivotal role of social behaviour in the hypothesized relationship between social cognition and social adjustment can be established by examining links between behaviour and social cognitive functioning, and between behaviour and social adjustment. Establishing these links is important because they have implications for interventions, such as social skills training and behavioural modification. Association does not, however, indicate a direction of cause, nor whether a causative relationship exists at all: the nature of the relation-ship can be established only by closely examining the cognitive antecedents and social consequences of behaviour. Inferences can also be made in the light of social ecological factors such as the context within which assessments are based.

Conclusions

A social cognitive model of adjustment attempts to explain the social adjustment of children with LD in terms of social perception, social cognition, or interpersonal understanding, variables mediating the relationship between LD and social behaviour and adjustment. According to Baron and Kenny (1986), a mediating variable is one that is assumed to account for a significant part of the relationship between an independent variable and a dependent variable. The presence or absence of LD in this case can be considered as an independent vari-able, with the dependent variables being social cognitive functioning, behaviour and social adjustment. In this model, social cognitive func-tioning (including social perception) mediates LD status and social behaviour, and social behaviour can also be considered as mediating the relationship between LD and social adjustment. Confirmation of the role of hypothesized mediator variables in the model can be made only in the light of empirical observations, such as correlation or regressions for each link in the model. It is in this regard that, in this book, various studies on each aspect of the social functioning of chil-dren with LD are discussed in relation to the evidence they provide for the model.

Chapter 2

Social functioning and adjustment in the school setting

An understanding of the relationship between social functioning and adjustment requires consideration of the role of contextual variables in determining both the nature and manifestation of such a relationship. The theoretical framework for this arises in part from Bronfenbrenner's (1979) ecological model of human development, in so far as the setting for a child's social interactions influences the nature of his or her social functioning.

On this basis, social functioning and associated social adjustment are considered to be influenced by both the characteristics of the child and the characteristics of the setting. Settings or contexts may vary in how they stimulate modes of functioning, with certain skills being promoted in one context and other skills in different contexts. Since a large portion of children's time is spent in school, this is an ideal environment in which to conduct studies of social functioning and adjustment. Of particular interest are relationships with peers (Asher and Parker, 1989). There has been general agreement in the literature that peer relations afford children the opportunity, among other benefits, to acquire interpersonal skills (Piaget, 1965; Youniss, 1980).

In this chapter, the social ecology of the school is first examined for its implications for social cognitive development of children with LD, with particular reference to peer relationships. What type of school setting promotes optimal development: the integrated mainstream setting or the segregated special school? This issue is discussed in relation to developmental outcomes in social functioning, and in relation to how each type of setting addresses the social-emotional needs of children with LD. Arguments in favour of and against each of these settings are examined in the light of research. Various aspects of the social adjustment of these children are then examined and discussed. Finally, the theoretical and practical implications of research findings are discussed.

The social ecology of the school

The extent to which the school setting may facilitate social relationships, and thereby stimulate the social cognitive and behavioural development of children with LD, is largely mediated by its social ecology. For example, with whom do children with LD interact? What activities take place and under what conditions? What functional demands are brought to bear on the participants in these contexts, and how do children with LD cope with the demands?

As a social environment, the school can vary in terms of (a) opportunities to interact with peers; (b) the characteristics of those with whom the child interacts, including whether they mostly constitute other children with LD or non-LD children; (c) the dispositions, including attitudes and behaviour, of others towards the children with LD; and (d) the demand or expectation for academic or social achievement. These characteristics differ between integrated settings and segregated special settings.

In most cases the characteristics of the social environment of schools in which children with LD may be placed are a policy issue for local educational committees. For example, in Britain following the 1981 Education Act that made provision for integration of children with LD into mainstream schools, various models of provision have been implemented. These range from partial integration by way of a special unit set up in a mainstream school, to full integration, whereby children with LD attend the same classes as their non-LD peers. These contexts offer different levels of opportunities for children with LD to interact with others, and with peers who may be more socially competent. Other children may also still be provided for in segregated special schools, and the question of interest is really whether any type of integration offers a more positive outcome than segregation.

Integrated mainstream versus special school

The debates that have surrounded efforts at integrating children with LD into mainstream schools reflects the importance attached to environmental factors, specifically the social context. In Britain, such efforts came to the fore with the Education Act of 1981 following the Warnock Report (1978).

Arguments in favour of integrating children with LD into mainstream schools have been put forward based on apparent benefits in social functioning and adjustment (Demchak and Drinkwater, 1992). It has been argued, for example, that integrated settings offer children with LD the opportunity for:

- more appropriate interactions and increased self initiations in social situations (Esposito and Peach, 1983);

- the development of more complex language and communication skills (Guralnick, 1978);
- decreased inappropriate play (Guralnick, 1981).

Thus, in integrated settings, children with LD can acquire social skills and age-appropriate behaviours through observational learning from normally developing peers, and such contexts offer opportunities for generalization of those skills (Templeman *et al.*, 1989). These benefits have also been cited by parents of children with disabilities who consider integrated programmes to be more stimulating (Guralnick, 1990) and offering more positive social outcomes (Palmer *et al.*, 1998) than segregated ones.

In terms of social adjustment, it is argued that integration into a mainstream school reduces the stigma of a segregated setting and increases the level of acceptance of children with LD by their non-LD peers (Zigler and Hall, 1986). Non-LD children may not only help identify age-appropriate valid activities, but also develop increased understanding of, sensitivity to, and tolerance for individual differences. In this way, non-LD children would develop and display favourable attitudes towards peers with LD as a result of direct contact with these children (Esposito and Peach, 1983).

Alternative views for segregation include the argument that some children with LD may need protection from the pressures of social demands that obtain in mainstream settings. The strains of these pressures might inhibit the development or display of social skills the mainstream setting is purported to promote. One particular argument is that children with LD (and indeed other types of disabilities as well) may suffer as they may be rejected by mainstream peers. Such rejection, it has been argued, is likely to arise from exposure of non-LD children to 'negative' behavioural characteristics of children with LD, thus increasing the social isolation of the latter (Gottlieb, 1981). Children with LD in mainstream settings can in this way have their self-confidence eroded and be subjected to greater anxiety.

There have been a number of studies examining the effectiveness of integration in terms of social and psychological outcomes. Two types of study are of interest here:

- those focusing on the effect of the integrated setting on social functioning of children with LD;
- those examining the social adjustment of these children as reflected in their social experiences in such settings.

Some studies on social functioning have focused on changes or differences in behaviour of children with LD in mainstream versus integrated settings, while others have looked at patterns of interaction amongst children with LD, and between them and non-LD peers. Studies on the social adjustment of children with LD in mainstream settings have looked at such issues as:

- their sociometric status or levels of social acceptance by non-LD peers;
- their social experiences, including bullying and victimization;
- their self-perceptions and social-emotional adjustment.

These issues are considered in this chapter in relation to how they reflect on the relative impact of segregated versus integrated settings on children with LD.

Type of school setting and social functioning

There is some evidence that, in general, the social context can have an effect on the social behaviour of children (e.g. Goldman, 1981; Guralnick, 1981). Goldman observed that young children in mixed-age groups played in a maturer manner than did those in same-age groups, so that the presence of older children apparently had this 'positive' effect on the behaviour of other children in the group. It has been argued, on the basis of such findings, that children with LD would similarly benefit from exposure to normal play and learning experiences in integrated settings, and so acquire more mature and socially appropriate forms of behaviour (Guralnick, 1981, 1986). Studies testing this assumption have therefore examined differences in the types and patterns of behaviour of children with LD in integrated compared with segregated settings.

Changes in behaviour

A number of studies have shown beneficial effects of integration (e.g. Guralnick, 1976; Guralnick and Groom, 1988; Sloper and Tyler, 1992). Buysse and Bailey (1993) reviewed the literature comparing outcomes for young children with disabilities in integrated and segregated settings, across 22 studies. Their meta-analysis indicated that, although children's developmental outcomes over time did not vary as a function of integrated versus segregated placements, integration was generally beneficial for children with disabilities in terms of social and other behavioural outcomes. Social benefits included:

- more time looking at and being in proximity of peers;
- higher rates of peer-related behaviour;
- more positive interactions with peers and an increase in positive interactions over time;

- higher levels of social participation and more verbalizations directed towards peers.

Other behavioural outcomes documented in the studies reviewed by Buysse and Bailey included observations that integrated children with disabilities exhibited less object-directed behaviour; on the other hand, when they played with objects such as toys, they did so more appropriately and at increased levels of sophistication.

Buysse and Bailey concluded that the findings suggested that integrated environments maintain developmental growth and provide a social context for facilitating peer-related behaviours among young children with disabilities. In addition, such contexts were considered to provide the opportunity to develop the skills of playing with toys and other materials, which – for young children – could be viewed as precursors to positive social interactions and relations with other children. For example, the type of setting had apparently affected the *cognitive* level of play with toys, with functional and constructive play being associated more with the integrated setting.

Similar gains in social and cognitive functioning have been reported in other studies (Fryxell and Kennedy, 1995; Kennedy *et al.*, 1997; Sloper and Tyler, 1992). Sloper and Tyler found that children with LD improved in concentration, cognitive development, and language in the mainstream school setting compared with the special school setting. A study by Kennedy *et al.* (1997) found that children with disabilities in inclusive settings provided and received higher proportions of social support (indicating social reciprocity) than did those in special settings.

There are, however, some indications that the benefits of integration may depend on the level of inclusion as well as on the level of functioning of children with LD. Mills *et al.* (1998) reported a study in which three levels of inclusion were compared on cognitive and language development of pre-school children with disabilities. The children were assigned randomly to special education only, integrated special education, and mainstream placements. Mills and colleagues found that differential benefits were received from these placements by higher and lower functioning children: relatively higher functioning children with disabilities benefited more from integrated special education placement, while those children with relatively lower functioning benefited more from special education-only classes and mainstream classes. Such differential effects of integration suggest that the impact of this social context may not be generalizable to all children with LD.

The impact of improvements in behaviour of children with LD on the quality of peer relations in integrated settings is also not so straightforward. For example:

'... *although young children with disabilities have more opportunities to interact with competent social partners in integrated settings and have a tendency to do so with greater frequency, they may be unable to achieve and maintain more sophisticated levels of play that ultimately lead to the development of friendship and true integration'.*

(Buysse and Bailey, 1993, p. 452)

Buysse and Bailey pointed out that some studies in their review had revealed the potential for unoccupied or isolated play among children with disabilities in integrated settings. Such observations lead us to consider the patterns of behaviour of children with LD in integrated versus segregated settings and their implications for the social adjustment of these children.

Patterns of interaction and social relations

Studies indicate that children with LD experience interactions with teachers that are qualitatively and quantitatively different from those experienced by non-LD peers (Pearl *et al.*, 1986). In some studies, children with LD have been reported to interact more with teachers (Roberts *et al.*, 1991; Siperstein and Goding, 1983). Others have reported students with LD to interact with teachers at much lower rates than other students (Mcintosh *et al.*, 1993).

While these contrasting findings make the patterns of interaction unclear, it seems that the nature of behaviours observed could be a significant factor. Where children with LD were observed to interact more with teachers than did their non-LD peers, the teachers tended to be more directive and corrective towards the children with LD (Siperstein and Goding, 1983), which may reflect difficulties in attending to tasks by those children. Other studies of classroom behaviour, for example, have consistently found children with LD to be more off-task or distractible (Bryan, 1974a; Feagans and McKinney, 1981; Roberts *et al.*, 1991). There are also some indications that teachers are more likely to criticize children with LD, or to ignore their initiations (Bryan, 1974a).

Pupil–teacher interactions

Patterns of interaction between teachers and children with LD are important because they have implications for the children's peer relations.

First, if children with LD spend more time with teachers they presumably have less time available to interact with peers. Interaction with teachers is, however, more likely to occur in the context of curriculum-based activities and to be adult-initiated.

A second, and perhaps more likely, effect on peer relations was observed by Lynas (1986), who pointed out that the constant support of teachers or other adults required by children with LD can be a source of resentment for their non-LD peers – with potentially negative effects on the social relations of children with LD. It is also likely that the behaviour of teachers towards children with LD can have an effect on how non-LD peers respond to them. It has been suggested that teachers can at times pay undue attention to characteristics that emphasize how different children with LD are (Weinstein *et al.*, 1982). Such attention can inadvertently convey negative regard or implied expectation of lower or inferior performance by children with LD, which can affect their social status and may even encourage bullying by peers (DfEE, 2000). Thus, teachers' implied negative perceptions of children with LD may be communicated to classmates.

Pupil–pupil interactions
A number of studies have found no differences between children with LD and other children in the amount of time spent in interaction with classmates (Pearl *et al.*, 1986; Roberts *et al.*, 1991). Studies of integrating children into mainstream schools, in terms of patterns of interaction with peers, have documented both positive and negative outcomes.

In terms of positive outcomes, Sloper and Tyler (1992) reported a study in which five children from a school for children with severe learning difficulties were placed in local mainstream schools. They examined, amongst other things, changes in the children's behaviour, peers' behaviour towards the children, and the social contacts of the children. The children with LD were reported to show improvement in independence and self-help skills. It was noted that the mainstream school routine allowed and encouraged considerably more independence than did the special school routine, in such matters as dining, toileting and playtime. Positive attitudes and behaviour of mainstream children towards children with LD were also reported in terms of help, friendship, and acceptance.

Kennedy *et al.* (1997) compared the social relationships of two groups of children with severe disabilities aged 12–14 years: one group was fully integrated in general education classrooms; the other group was supported in special classrooms. Findings indicated that children in the integrated general education setting had more social benefits than did children in the special setting. In addition to providing and receiving higher proportions of social support, the former were observed to interact more frequently with peers without disabilities and had larger and more durable networks of peers without disabilities. Similar findings have been reported regarding pre-school children (Guralnick and Groom, 1988; Jenkins *et al.*, 1989), and middle (elementary) school children (Fryxell and Kennedy, 1995).

However, the reported positive outcomes in social relations may apply only to children with severe disabilities and not to those with mild or moderate disabilities. A number of studies have reported children of pre-school and junior school age with a range of mild to moderate disabilities to interact less frequently with mainstream peers (Cavallaro and Porter, 1980; Martlew and Cooksey, 1989). Mainstream children have also been observed to stay in closer proximity to other mainstream children than to such children with disabilities (Porter *et al.*, 1978).

Other studies have found no differences in both the amount and quality of social behaviours of children with LD in integrated and special (segregated) settings. Martlew and Hodson (1991) compared the social behaviour of children in two schools, one mainstream with an integrated resource unit for children with mild LD, the other a special school. A group of children with LD from the special school and another group of children with LD from the mainstream school, matched with mainstream children for age and sex, took part in the study. Observations were made of children in the playground and their social proximity, and positive and negative behaviours were categorized. In addition, self-reports on social relationships were collected from the children in the mainstream school. The findings indicated no differences in the amount of social contact children with LD had in the mainstream and special school, nor were there significant differences in total positive and negative behaviours.

Martlew and Hodson (1991) also found that mainstream children played significantly less frequently with children with LD, and this was more marked in the older than in the younger children. Self-reports from children in the integrated school indicated that the children with LD were teased or bullied more and made fewer friends than did the mainstream children.

Thus, the integrated mainstream setting apparently did not have any advantages over the special setting in terms of patterns of social behaviour of children with mild to moderate LD. Perhaps more significantly, the integrated setting seemed to have had some negative effect on the social experiences of the children with LD.

Conclusion
Studies on social outcomes of integrated versus segregated settings appear equivocal. A number have shown positive effects of integration relative to segregation. In particular, improved behaviour has been observed in children with LD as a result of integration in some studies, while other studies found no differences or some negative outcomes. Similar findings have been reported regarding patterns of interaction.

These variations appear to be a function of the severity of disability of the integrated children. Children with mild to moderate LD may not be included spontaneously in the social activities of their non-LD peers, and may not generally be socially accepted in mainstream settings. As children in integrated programmes tend to be those with mild to moderate disabilities, this has implications for the psychological well-being of the majority of children with LD in mainstream settings. Social acceptance by the peer group is an aspect of the social ecology that has important consequences for general social and emotional adjustment of children in general (Parker and Asher, 1987). For example, lack of acceptance by peers may mean isolation and loneliness for a child, and may undermine feelings of self-worth. Thus, the social adjustment of children with LD has a lot to do with the quality of their social relations. A significant aspect of this relates to their personal experiences in such settings. These include social and emotional experiences related to self-perceptions and feelings of well-being.

Social adjustment: experiences of children with LD

Various types of social experience may influence the social adjustment of children with LD in mainstream settings. These can be considered to occur at two levels. One of these relates to the general 'climate' or social ecology and involves how other children, mostly non-LD peers, relate to children with LD as demonstrated by attitudes and behaviour directed towards them. Attitudes can be determined by examining the social status and acceptance of children with LD, while experiences of victimization and bullying are good indices of adjustment problems for both the perpetrators and those at the receiving end.

The other level relates to the impact on individual children. Self-perception is one example of an outcome as it relates to personal feelings of self-worth and has implications for social efficacy in interpersonal relations. Other experiences relate to social emotional attributes, such as feelings of coherence, companionship, or loneliness. These experiences will be discussed in the context of integrated settings for children with LD.

Social status and acceptance

While some social benefits of integration have been documented for children with disabilities (e.g. Buysse and Bailey, 1993; Sloper and Tyler, 1992), findings reflecting social status and acceptance in such settings have been rather mixed. Several studies have indicated that children with LD or intellectual disabilities in integrated school settings tend to have lower social status (Bryan, 1974b, 1976; MacMillan and Morrison, 1984; Nabuzoka and Smith, 1993; Ochoa and Palmer, 1991; Ochoa and Olivarez, 1995; Stone and LaGreca, 1990; Swanson and Malone, 1992; Taylor *et al.*, 1987). Children with LD in these studies received fewer positive and more negative nominations. Rejection has been found to be especially strong for girls with LD in some studies (Kistner and Gatlin, 1989a,b; Scranton and Ryckman, 1979). Other studies similarly found that children with LD were frequently rated less positively than were their classmates; they were often less popular, more rejected, or more ignored (Bruininks, 1978; Garrett and Crump, 1980; Horowitz, 1981). Taylor *et al.* (1987) studied the social adaptation of mainstreamed children with mild intellectual disabilities, by comparing them with a matched sample of regular education students. The children with mild disabilities were not only rejected by their peers, they also reported significantly more dissatisfaction and anxiety about their peer relations than did the non-LD children. These findings suggest particular social adjustment problems for children with disabilities that are an outcome of, or are at least perpetuated by, integration.

Some studies, on the other hand, have found no significant differences in attitudes towards peers with LD, between mainstreamed and non-mainstreamed children (Archie and Sherril, 1989), nor in proportions of children with LD and non-LD children across accepted and unpopular sociometric groups (Juvonen and Bear, 1992).

Such contrasting findings raise questions as to the actual effects of integration on attitudes of non-LD children towards children with LD. It may be that the findings reflect variations in the degree of integration. Some research indicates that attitudes of non-LD children towards those with LD could be enhanced if there were more social interactions between them (Favazza and Odom, 1997; Newberry and Parish, 1987; Townsend *et al.*, 1993; Voeltz, 1980, 1982). This is more difficult to achieve by mere placement of children with LD in integrated units within the ordinary school (Taylor *et al.*, 1987).

Favazza and Odom (1997) reported a study in which groups of kindergarten-age (pre-school) children with different levels of contact with other children with disabilities were compared on their acceptance of people with disabilities. One group, the high-contact group, participated in a programme designed to promote such acceptance; meanwhile, a low-contact group had incidental contact with children with disabilities; and a no-contact group had neither direct nor indirect contact with children with disabilities. Initially, all participants had low levels of acceptance, but after programme treatment significant gains in levels of acceptance were found only in the high-contact group.

Positive effects of contact seem to apply to children with severe LD and not those with mild to moderate LD (Janney *et al.*, 1995). One explanation is that while non-LD peers may be 'forgiving' towards children with severe LD, and thus make allowances for differences in behaviour (see McHugh, 1970, on deviance and expectations), differences with those with lesser LD may not be so apparent. Non-LD children may thus have the same socio-behavioural expectations for the children with mild to moderate LD as they do for non-LD friends such that, when the child with a disability fails to live up to

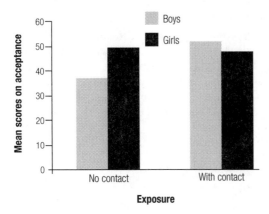

Figure 2.1 *Mean sccores on acceptance of children with LD across exposure (contact versus no contact) and gender (Source: Nabuzoka and Rønning, 1997: 110)*

expectations, he or she is rejected or isolated (Siperstein *et al.*, 1980). Newberry and Parish's (1987) findings seem to support this view: children who had interacted with peers with different types of disabilities showed more positive attitudes towards the children with all types of disabilities except those with LD (i.e. those whose handicap was not so obvious).

In the light of the above, Nabuzoka and Rønning (1997) examined the social acceptance of a group of Zambian primary school children with LD (identified to have mild to moderate intellectual disabilities) by two groups of non-LD peers. The two latter groups were from the same school as the children with LD. However, one group was in direct contact with the children with LD over a period of six months while the other was not. During this period, structured activities were applied when the group of non-LD children interacted with children with LD. The question of interest was whether non-LD children who had the opportunity to interact with children with disabilities would show more acceptance than non-LD children who had not interacted with them. Both groups of non-LD children were aware of the status of children with LD.

Nabuzoka and Rønning found that non-LD boys who had been in contact with children with LD had more positive attitudes than boys who had no direct contact, while no exposure effects were observed amongst girls. Gender differences amongst non-LD children who had contact with peers with disabilities were not significant. Amongst the non-LD children who had no contact with children with LD, girls had the more positive attitudes. These findings are depicted in Figure 2.1. The treatment effects for boys, though not for girls, were consistent with earlier findings by Newberry and Parish (1987).

These findings suggest an interaction of two factors: gender and exposure or level of integration. They indicate, for example, that boys in general may initially have more negative attitudes towards peers with disabilities than do girls. The findings also suggest that boys can nevertheless develop more positive attitudes when given the opportunity to interact with peers with LD. Similar studies have documented significant sex differences with girls having more accepting attitudes than boys (Rothlisberg *et al.*, 1994; Townsend *et al.*, 1993; Voeltz, 1980, 1982). However, while exposure may serve to improve the attitude of boys, this seems to have little effect on girls' attitude. The significance of considering gender differences in studying the social functioning of children with LD is discussed further in Chapter 7.

Research findings indicating more acceptance with contact are contrary to the view that exposure of non-LD children to behavioural characteristics of children with LD is likely to increase the social isolation of the latter (Gottlieb, 1981). Should this be the case, the non-LD children who have had contact with children with LD should have more negative attitudes than those who may have had no contact. However, the designs of the studies by Favazza and Odom (1997) and by Nabuzoka and Rønning (1997) make interpretation difficult. In both studies, some of the non-LD children whose attitudes were being examined were involved in intervention programmes partly aimed at increasing positive attitudes (see also Rønning and Nabuzoka, 1993). This makes it unclear as to whether the observed effects were due to simple exposure of such children or to their being part of the intervention programme.

It is also possible that increased positive attitudes associated with exposure to children with LD could reflect decreased inappropriate behaviours by the latter, possibly resulting from exposure to more competent peers and/or to the demands of the integrated setting. This is supported by the study by Rønning and Nabuzoka (1993) which reported increased sociometric status of children with LD associated with increased pro-social behaviours. That study is discussed further in Chapter 5 in the context of the relationship between behavioural attributes of children with LD and their overall social adjustment.

However, the relatively negative attitudes of the children not in contact with children with LD would indicate prior negative expectations, and not observed behaviour as such, since this group of children would not have been involved in direct social interaction (Favazza and Odom, 1997; Nabuzoka and Rønning, 1997). Support for the hypothesis linking positive attitudes to development of socially appropriate behaviour by children with LD would need to show that the attitudes of the non-LD children who were in contact with peers with disabilities became less accepting on initial contact, and then improved as a result of behavioural changes in the children with LD.

What is clearly indicated by these studies is that attitudes may be modified by regular contact with children with LD. Mere placement of such children in units within integrated settings may not necessarily lead to improved social acceptance. Deliberate efforts are required to ensure that they are in *actual contact* with non-LD children. In addition, other variables such as gender may affect the level of acceptance. But whether changes in attitudes by non-LD children are a result of observed changes in the behaviour of children with LD is a question that needs to be addressed separately. One way of doing that is to examine *how* peers perceive the behaviour of children with LD, and whether such perceptions are associated with how they relate to such children. This issue is addressed in Chapter 5.

Conclusion

Research on social status and acceptance of children with LD by non-LD peers in integrated school settings generally indicates negative outcomes for children with LD. The latter tend to have lower social status and are less well accepted by peers. However, such attitudes may relate to the severity of the presenting difficulties of children with LD; those with more severe difficulties being more accepted than those with less severe problems. The amount of contact between children with LD and other children, and the gender of the children, are other seemingly important factors. Increased contact appears to lead to the development of more positive attitudes, especially for boys and when accompanied by an intervention programme designed to increase levels of social interaction. Where such intervention is lacking, children with LD may be considered to be at risk for adjustment problems. One indicator of social adjustment related to social acceptance is how other children actually behave towards them. For example, children who are not well integrated in peer groups may be susceptible to bullying and victimization.

Bullying and victimization

In school, children who are alone at playtime or do not have many friends run an increased risk of being bullied (Olweus, 1991; Thompson and Arora, 1991). Children with LD are thus vulnerable to bullying and victimization because they lack protective peer relationships, and several studies have indeed shown this.

O'Moore and Hillery (1989) gave questionnaires to 783 pupils, including some with LD, in four schools in Dublin. They found that children with LD (those in remedial classes) reported themselves to be victims of bullying more often than did the other children. This was especially true of frequent bullying (defined as once a week or more), which was reported by 12 per cent of children with LD compared with 7 per cent of non-LD children. Differences in bullying behaviour were not so obvious or consistent.

As pointed out earlier, the study by Martlew and Hodson (1991) – which used interviews with children and observations to investigate social relationships – also found that children with LD in an integrated school were teased/bullied more and made fewer friends than did mainstream (non-LD) children. Similarly, Nabuzoka and Smith (1993) looked at social relationships of children in two primary schools with integrated resources. They also interviewed mainstream (non-LD) children and children with moderate LD. The study looked at the children's perceptions of which of their classmates best fitted a number of behavioural descriptions, including those of a bully and a victim. Children with LD were very much more likely than non-LD children to be selected as victims. A larger proportion (33 per cent) of children with LD were thought to be victims compared with non-LD children, of whom only 8 per cent were victims. Again, selection as bullies did not differ significantly between children with LD and other children.

Thompson *et al.* (1994) aimed to discover whether children defined as having special needs really did suffer more from bullying than matched non-LD children in the mainstream part of the school. Detailed interviews were conducted in three primary (8–11) schools and five secondary (11–16) schools with 186 children and their teachers. Ninety-three of the children were classified as having special educational needs, and the other 93 were mainstream children with no special educational needs; each child with special needs was paired with another mainstream child who had the same age, gender, ethnicity, year group and school. The interview schedule asked each child some general questions about life in school, friendships, and experiences of being bullied or bullying others. Teachers who knew the children with special needs best in each school were also interviewed, covering questions similar to those asked of the children.

Thompson and colleagues reported that the children with special needs were generally much more likely to be bullied than were the mainstream children. About two-thirds of the children with special needs reported being bullied, compared with only a quarter of the other children. It was also found that experiences of being bullied were related to the type of special educational needs of the children: proportionally more children with moderate LD were victimized than were children with mild LD. The children with special needs also reported themselves to have fewer friends than their mainstream counterparts. Teachers' views were reasonably consistent with the findings from the children in recognizing the likelihood of children with special needs being bullied, but they tended to underestimate the frequency of bullying compared with the pupils' self-reports.

Conclusion

It seems that children with LD in integrated mainstream school settings are much more likely to have negative experiences of being bullied and victimized. They are therefore more at risk for adjustment problems associated with such experiences. Research on typically developing (non-LD) children has shown that peer victimization and school maladjustment are related. Compared with unvictimized classmates, victimized children in school are lonelier (Boulton and Underwood, 1992; Kochenderfer and Ladd, 1996) and less happy (Boulton and Underwood, 1992). Victimized children also display lower levels of school liking and higher levels of school avoidance (Kochenderfer and Ladd, 1996).

Kochenderfer and Ladd (1996) studied 200 children aged 5 and 6 years (105 males and 95 females) and explored the hypothesis that early peer victimization has a negative impact on children's school adjustment and, in particular, leads to negative school attitudes, perceptions, and feelings. Findings indicated that children who were victimized were significantly more lonely, were more school avoidant, and liked school less. It was also suggested that peer victimization was a precursor of some school adjustment problems: victimized children tended to become more lonely and school avoidant *after* they were victimized by peers, and victimization was a significant predictor of loneliness and school avoidance. Such experiences are also likely to have an effect on the children's self-esteem, which may further undermine their social functioning.

Self-perceptions and social–emotional adjustment

One argument for integration, and against segregation, is that segregation has the effect of labelling children with LD, with negative effects on self-perception (Coleman, 1983; Kistner *et al.*, 1987). However, some research evidence has tended to suggest that children with LD placed in segregated classes have higher self-esteem than do those in regular integrated classes (Coleman, 1983). That is consistent with the view that self-perceptions of children with LD depend mainly on the targets with which they compare themselves (Grolnick and Ryan, 1990). In this respect, children with LD who attend segregated settings can feel more positive about themselves because their salient reference group consists of others with LD like themselves. Children with LD in integrated settings, on the other hand, may have their self-esteem undermined by comparisons with more competent peers.

It has been suggested that the level of integration, whether part time or full time, may be relevant. According to social comparison theory (Goethals, 1986; Wills, 1981) and reference group theory (Hyman and Singer, 1976), children with LD who are integrated into mainstream classes for part of a school day should be much more likely to show gains in self-esteem than children in segregated classes. The argument is that exposure to both LD peers and non-LD peers should enable children with LD to make selective use of multiple comparison groups in ways that can bolster self-esteem. Thus:

> '... *the general self-esteem of children with LD can be maintained both by the sense of belonging to a "normal" social group and by comparisons with nondisabled classmates in domains not affected by their disabilities, while academic self-esteem can be maintained by comparisons with special education classmates in this domain.*'

(Butler and Marinov-Glassman, 1994, p. 326)

To test this hypothesis, Butler and Marinov-Glassman obtained measures of perceived competence and perceived achievement of three groups of Israeli students. One group comprised children with LD attending special schools, another group comprised children with LD attending special classes in regular schools, and another group comprised low achievers in regular classes. The findings were that, after the early elementary school grades, perceived competence in scholastic, social and general competence was higher among the special-school group than among the special-class and low-achieving groups. These findings were contrary to what would be expected on the basis of social comparison and reference group theories, and were taken to suggest that exposure to more competent peers somewhat undermined perceived competence of the special-class and low-achieving groups. In addition, once at an age for a developed capacity for normal social comparison, the children with LD in special classes tended to compare themselves primarily with non-LD peers, thus reflecting negatively on their self-worth.

It would appear, therefore, that integrating children with LD into mainstream settings may not be in the best interests of these children, as far as the development of positive self-concept and esteem is concerned, as such contexts may serve only to undermine any sense of self-efficacy that they might have. But such negative effects may mostly relate to perceived limitations in scholastic competence, and may not apply where integration is accompanied by interventions addressing such limitations. Some studies have suggested that where inclusive practices result in academic gains, similar affective gains may also be observed. Banerji and Dailey (1995), for example, reported a study in which an inclusion programme was examined for its outcomes on students who were normally achieving or who showed specific LD. Their findings indicated that students with LD made some academic and affective gains at a pace comparable to the normally achieving students, and these gains were accompanied by improved self-esteem and, in some cases, improved motivation by students with LD.

Conclusion

Self-perceptions, such as perceived competence in scholastic and social domains, are important because they involve an appraisal of one's capabilities and limitations and so can be said to guide one's behaviour. However, social functioning can be influenced by various factors. There is now extensive research indicating that children with LD are at risk for several other aspects of socio-emotional maladjustment in integrated settings. Compared with non-LD peers, children with LD report higher levels of loneliness and lower levels of coherence (Margalit, 1998; Margalit and Efrati, 1996; Tur-Kaspa *et al.*, 1999), higher anxiety (Fisher *et al.*, 1996), more stress (Wenz-Gross and Siperstein, 1998) and greater feelings of depression (Heinman and Margalit, 1998).

To the extent that such experiences are associated with the mainstream settings, integration of children with LD into mainstream schools could be associated with social adjustment problems. These at the very least need to be weighed against the benefits of integration. But if one accepts the premise that social functioning is a function of both contextual and subject (in this case, children with LD) variables, a more positive approach would be to identify and address contextual contingencies as well as characteristics of children with LD that contribute to such adjustment problems. Intervention aimed at maximizing benefits of integration can as a result be informed of the factors that contribute to such adjustment problems.

Summary and conclusions

The social ecology of the school has important implications for the social functioning and adjustment of children with LD. Research has generally shown integrated settings to be more beneficial than segregated settings for children with LD in terms of social and behavioural outcomes, and gains in social cognitive functioning. Such benefits may, however, not be of sufficient magnitude for the development of positive social relations for these children.

Social outcomes in terms of patterns of social interaction, social networks and acceptance appear to be only somewhat more positive for children with severe disabilities and not for those with mild to moderate disabilities. As most children integrated into mainstream schools tend to fall into the latter group, the majority of those children may not experience the positive social outcomes of integration.

The differential effects of integration appear to be more marked in older than younger children, while gender may also be a factor. In addition, the degree of exposure or contact between children with LD and non-LD children seems to be significant in the social acceptance of children with LD.

One outcome of lack of peer acceptance and the resultant social isolation is the increased risk of being bullied and victimized by peers. Children with LD appear particularly vulnerable in this regard. These and other difficulties related to peer acceptance constitute adjustment problems generally faced by these children in mainstream settings. The problems may be manifested in loneliness, unhappiness and negative school attitudes, perceptions and feelings. Functional limitations and problems in social relations, which may be highlighted in integrated settings, may also undermine self-esteem as well as the emotional adjustment of children with LD. These adjustment problems need to be weighed against the benefits of integration.

Of primary concern is the need to determine ways in which positive outcomes of the school setting can be maximized while minimizing the negative outcomes. In a number of instances such efforts can build on existing contingencies in the functioning of children with LD. For example, a focus on enhancing increases in appropriate social behaviours can lead to more positive and sustained social interactions, thereby decreasing social isolation. Such efforts require identification of aspects of the integrated setting that promote improvements in social behaviours. They also require identification of the factors that lead non-LD children to respond negatively to children with LD.

Similarly, aspects of the integrated setting that contribute to social emotional difficulties of children with LD can be identified and then addressed through particular adjustments in either structural or functional orientations. For example, it is clear that activities in mainstream settings that involve greater contact between children with LD and non-LD peers are likely to lead to more acceptance of children with LD, while also enhancing their self-esteem.

A fuller understanding of factors associated with social adjustment also requires an examination of the children's functional characteristics and how these interact with social ecological factors to account for social adjustment. Such a concern is consistent with the view that social adjustment is to a large extent a function of both contextual variables and characteristics of the individual.

It is argued in the following chapters that social cognitive abilities of children with LD are associated with their behavioural dispositions, and that these contribute significantly to the children's social adjustment in mainstream integrated settings. Simply put, children with LD socialize and interact with others in a manner consistent with their level of social understanding. Their behavioural skills are obviously important. Their behavioural responses in turn set the tone for how others respond. Problems in social relations can therefore reflect the quality of their behaviour, which in turn is influenced by their level of social understanding.

Chapter 3

Social perception: recognition of person and contextual cues

Successful social interaction involves making judgements about situations and responding appropriately. This entails recognizing cues such as facial and bodily expressions, and being able to interpret them correctly. It is also likely that as children get older, the ability to decode more subtle aspects of bodily postures and facial expressions becomes more important. In addition to such non-verbal cues, situational or contextual cues are also important in determining the tone of social interaction. The ability to decode social cues from non-verbal behaviour is therefore a significant element of an individual's overall ability to understand his or her social environment.

Children and adolescents with learning disabilities (LD) have been reported to exhibit a reduced ability to come to terms with the non-verbal aspects of communication (Johnson and Myklebust, 1967; Rourke, 1989). This could partly explain their difficulties in social relations with non-LD peers (Nabuzoka and Smith, 1993; Stone and LaGreca, 1990). Deficits in decoding social cues, for example, lead to an inability to understand when it is appropriate to perform certain behaviours, thus accounting for behaviours associated with peer rejection (Nabuzoka and Smith, 1993). For example, research indicates that some children, particularly sociometrically rejected children who are aggressive, may misinterpret cues of hostility or friendly intent (Dodge and Frame, 1982; Pellegrini, 1988).

Expressions of emotions are some of the basic components of non-verbal behaviour. In typically developing (non-LD) children, the ability to decode or understand emotions has been associated with social competence (Philippot and Fieldman, 1990), general social adjustment (Cook *et al.*, 1994), and high social status (Boyatzis and Satyaprasad, 1994; Hubbard and Coie, 1994; Walden and Field, 1990). Similarly, it has been suggested that inadequate social perceptual skills, including the failure to comprehend other people's affective states, lie behind the difficult social relationships experienced by children with LD (Myklebust, 1975). It has been suggested that deficits in interpreting the actions of others, including the ability to understand the emotions and feelings of others from facial expressions, is an aspect of non-verbal learning disabilities (Johnson and Myklebust, 1967; Rourke, 1989), and that these inabilities lead to disturbed social relationships and, probably, social isolation (Thompson, 1985).

This chapter examines and synthesizes the theoretical and empirical literature regarding the social perceptual abilities of children with LD. In a number of studies, children with LD have been found to perform worse than non-LD peers on tasks developed to measure an individual's ability to perceive and interpret emotions. The issues to be addressed in this chapter therefore include:

- the extent to which children with LD differ in their ability to identify such social cues accurately;
- the particular ways in which such differences may occur;
- how social perceptual skills are related to other aspects of social functioning such as behaviour;
- whether social perceptual deficits can explain interpersonal problems faced by some children with LD.

Three aspects of social perceptual functioning are discussed in turn: perception of expressions of emotions; perception of contextual and situational cues; and social inference and role-taking abilities.

Perception of expressions of emotions

Over the years, evidence has accumulated showing that in typically developing children, perception of affective states is present from a very early age (Harris, 1989; Hiatt *et al.*, 1979; Walker, 1982). By three years of age, normally developing children may be able to indicate emotions such as 'happy', 'sad', 'afraid', etc., from a series of photographed facial expressions (Izard, 1971). They are also able to make appropriate choices of schematically drawn faces to complete a picture of a person in situations that might lead the person to feel happy, sad, afraid or angry (Borke, 1971, 1973). In addition, young children are able to identify affective states on the basis of vocal as well as facial and bodily gestures, and this ability gradually improves with age (Dimitrovsky, 1964; Gross and Ballif, 1991).

Performance of groups of children with LD on tasks developed to measure an individual's ability to perceive and interpret emotions has been found to be degraded (Axelrod, 1982; Bryan, 1977; Wiig and Harris, 1974). It has been suggested that this indicates a social developmental lag in these children. Other researchers, on the other hand, have taken the view that a reduced ability to recognize social cues may reflect differences in general perceptual or cognitive development (Johnson and Myklebust, 1967; Wiig and Harris, 1974). Generally, there has been an apparent low-to-moderate relationship between performance on social cognitive tasks and the children's level of intelligence (Chandler, 1977; Shantz, 1983).

Studies have generally examined the ability to recognize affective states in relation to intellectual or learning disability, age, gender and type of emotion. Holder and Kirkpatrick (1991), for example, examined the accuracy and time required for children with LD and non-LD children to interpret emotions from facial expressions. Children with LD aged 8–10 years and 11–15 years, matched with non-LD children for age and sex, were presented with slides of faces expressing emotions of fear, sadness, surprise, anger, happiness, and disgust. The children had to select the expression appropriate to scenarios and labels presented from a pair of expressions shown simultaneously. Children with LD were found to be less accurate in interpreting emotion, and they spent more time identifying specific emotions. Younger children required more time to interpret the emotions of fear and anger; males spent more time interpreting happiness. Younger females with LD particularly displayed difficulty in interpretation, and older males with LD were often inaccurate, though rapid, interpreters of emotion.

Holder and Kirkpatrick's study focused on a single modality of facial expressions presented pictorially, and the recognition of facial expressions of emotions has been one of the most widely used measures of social perception. However, there are some indications that the ability to identify or recognize affective states may be related to the type of expression of the affective state, as well as intellectual or learning ability, age, gender, and the emotion itself (Nabuzoka and Smith, 1995). For example, some evidence suggests that children with LD, particularly boys, may not fully utilize facial expressions in their judgement of social interactions: they have been found to focus on motion cues and consequently neglect facial expressions and other non-verbal behaviours (Weiss, 1984). This may suggest that children with LD may perceive certain types of expressions more accurately than others. The question is whether differences between children with LD and non-LD children observed on one type of expressions are similarly reflected on another.

Nabuzoka and Smith (1995) examined the ability to identify emotions according to age and gender, as well as by the type of expression. Based on Spence's (1985) manual, *Social Skills Training with Children and Adolescents*, three tasks were used to assess perception of facial, postural and gestured cues. The children were presented with pictures depicting facial expressions and postures, and short video episodes of a child actor showing gestures. In addition to a comparison with non-LD children, a developmental perspective was taken by examining children with LD at different chronological ages (averages ages of 6.7 years, 9.2 years and 11.1 years). The non-LD children had an average age of 9.4 years. Some of the children were followed up a year later and reassessed on the same measures to provide a short-term longitudinal framework to supplement the cross-sectional data.

Consistent with earlier studies (e.g. Axelrod, 1982; Bryan, 1977; Holder and Kirkpatrick, 1991), Nabuzoka and Smith's study found that children with LD were less proficient on identifying emotions at all three age levels. Increased accuracy with age was observed, however, on most measures, and this trend was largely stable over the one-year period of the study. This seems to indicate that the skills required for these tasks are developmental, even for children with LD, and this is consistent with findings on non-LD children (Charlesworth and Kreutzer, 1973; Gross and Ballif, 1991). That children with LD perform at a lower level than age-matched non-LD children supports a 'social developmental lag' theory, and similar observations have been made in other studies (Gerber and Zinkgraf, 1982; Jackson *et al.*, 1987). Thus, whatever problems in social perception the children with LD may have cannot be explained solely on the basis of an *absolute* social perception deficit. Had this been the case, older children would not have performed better than younger ones.

However, while children with LD may improve with age, they may not necessarily catch up with non-LD peers. Nabuzoka and Smith (1995) found that, despite some high performances on some measures of emotion recognition, none of the scores of children with LD reached ceiling while some of those of the non-LD children did and were near those of adults. In addition, increased accuracy with age amongst children with LD was not observed on some measures, and some emotions were more accurately identified through certain expressions and not others. This suggests that the ability to identify emotions accurately at certain age levels may depend on either the emotion itself or the type of expression. In relation to the latter, Nabuzoka and Smith found that, while performance on the tasks requiring perception of facial and postural expressions did not greatly vary across disability/age levels, it was higher on gestures for all groups, including the youngest children with LD. This suggests that for this group of children, facial and postural expressions may not be as easy to decode as gestures (see Figure 3.1).

The differences in identifying emotions according to the type of expression and age of the subject indicates some developmental differentiation in the ability to decode types of social cues. The stages at which children with LD decode a given emotion may thus vary according to the type of expression. For example, decoding of the gesture for anger may occur earlier than that of the posture or facial expression for the same emotion. The latter cues could be said to be more subtle forms of non-verbal communication. Indeed, gestures are perhaps closer to being words than are facial expressions or postures.

It has long been noted that certain emotions can be identified at an earlier age in typically developing children (Borke, 1971, 1973; Gross

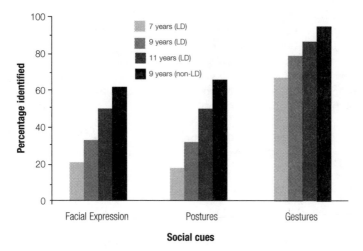

Figure 3.1 *Identification of emotions by type of expressive cue and age/disability (Nabuzoka and Smith, 1995)*

and Ballif, 1991; Izard, 1971). Similarly for children with LD and with respect to facial expressions, Nabuzoka and Smith (1995) found that the happy/pleased emotion tended to be accurately identified by most children at all ages. Fear was accurately identified by most of the older (average 9.2 years) and oldest (11.1 years) children with LD, as well as by non-LD children (9.4 years), but was one of the least identified for the youngest group (average 6.7 years), together with disgust, neutral and surprised emotions. In addition, while a moderate number of the youngest children with LD could also identify the expression of anger, a larger proportion of the older children with LD identified fear and surprise, which also seemed to be consolidated at the oldest age level.

Nabuzoka and Smith found that the interaction of emotion conveyed and type of expression was evident when the children's performance on facial expressions was compared with that on postures. For facial expressions, while fear was more accurately identified amongst the middle and oldest groups, sad and angry emotions did not seem to reflect a coherent age-related pattern, though the latter showed significant effects of age. On postures, however, and though there was no equivalent of the emotion of fear, perception of happy and sad emotions did significantly increase with age, unlike for facial expressions. Only the anger emotion was significantly related to age across the two measures. Performance on gestures was also different from the other two expressions. While overall age differences were observed across all emotions, the oldest group of children with LD and non-LD children not only identified gestures to a greater extent than either postures or facial expressions, but they also reached developmental ceiling on most emotions.

It could be argued that differences in performance might reflect the validity of the stimulus materials, rather than any variation in the development of relevant abilities. In the study by Nabuzoka and Smith (1995), for example, still photographs were used for identification of facial and postural cues while video episodes were used to assess perception of gestures. There have been some misgivings about the use of static pictures to represent emotions (Oster, 1981; Sherrod, 1981), and the lower performance by the children on postures and facial expressions might seem to support such views. There is, however, no definitive evidence that the stimulus materials alone can account for the differences in performance. Moreover, the robustness of communication of emotion via static photographs has been demonstrated (Wallbott, 1991). It has also been shown, for example, that children with intellectual disabilities are able to match schematic drawings of expressions of emotions with those enacted on video films (Hobson, 1986a). This would seem to indicate that children with LD would equally be competent in identifying emotions in the two mediums so long as the expression was within their repertoire. The uneven performance by children with LD across types of expressions is therefore more likely to be due to the relative ease of interpreting the expressions.

A number of studies have found no gender differences in the accuracy of identifying emotions from expressions (Brody, 1985; Gitter *et al.*, 1971; Nabuzoka and Smith, 1995), but others have reported differences (e.g. Hall, 1978). Even where no general gender differences have been observed, some differences seem to exist in specific areas. Nabuzoka and Smith found that, although there were no gender differences on most measures, girls were more accurate than boys in identifying the facial expression of disgust and the gesture for rejecting. This still leaves the question of gender differences inconclusive. At best, such equivocal findings indicate that gender differences are specific to particular emotions and/or expressions. Further studies could thus explore the specificity of gender differences on identification of emotions.

Conclusion

Accuracy in interpreting emotions through facial expression, postures and gestures is important for successful social interaction. Children with LD seem to be less adept at identifying these aspects of non-verbal behaviour, which could partly explain these children's difficulties in social relations. There are indications that this may be due to a general 'social developmental lag'. However, developmental differentiation according to particular social cues has also been evident. The ability to decode specific social cues would thus depend on the age of the subject, the emotion being expressed, and the type of expression. Thus, difficulties in identifying other people's affective states by children with LD may be more pronounced for more subtle cues such as postures, instead of gestures which may be relatively easier to decode.

A practical implication is that determining a child's developmental level with regard to his or her social perceptual abilities should include a consideration of these elements together. Social skill training should then take account of the specific manifestation of the social perceptual difficulties.

Perception of contextual or situational cues

Knowledge of the context or situation can provide important clues to another person's emotional state. Typically, both situational and expressive cues are available in a given social encounter and one may rely on one type of cue or the other.

Some empirical work suggests that both expressive and situational cues are used by typically developing children as sources of information in emotion judgement (Bretherton *et al.*, 1986; Gnepp, 1983). Research on the emotion knowledge of typically developing children has suggested that young pre-schoolers can infer basic emotions either from expressions or from situations (Denham and Couchoud, 1990), and that they can identify the linkage between emotional expressions, situations which unequivocally cause emotion (e.g. being happy to receive a gift), and the consequences of such emotional expressions (Denham and Couchoud, 1990; Strayer, 1986). It has also been shown that the ability to use the two sources of information are related. Thus, the child needs to be proficient in identifying emotional expressions before he or she can reliably associate them with certain situations (Denham and Couchoud, 1990).

The ability to identify the emotion related to the situation by typically developing children has been reported to increase with age and to vary with the particular emotion depicted (Gross and Ballif, 1991; Philippot and Fieldman, 1990). Such associations constitute knowledge of event scripts for specific emotions; for example, that one feels happy when receiving a gift (Bullock and Russell, 1986). In addition, the child may use either expressive and/or situational cues when inferring others' emotions, depending on the circumstances in which the emotion judgement is made (Camras, 1986). Developmental changes have also been observed in the relative weights assigned to expressive and situational cues, with reliance on situational cues increasing with age and reliance on expressive cues decreasing with age, especially where the two types of cues conflict (Gnepp, 1983; Hoffner and Badzinski, 1989; Reichenbach and Masters, 1983; Wiggers and van Lieshout, 1985).

Research on children with LD, however, has almost exclusively focused on one type of social cue, mostly expressive ones. There have been very few studies investigating the relative reliance on situational and expressive cues in the judgement of affective states of others by children with LD. Theoretically, examination of these children's abilities to integrate different types of cues is important in understanding their social development. For example, increased reliance with age of typically developing children on situational rather than expressive cues can be explained by the acquisition of display rules as children get older. These display rules are social conventions for modulating the expression of affect (Saarni, 1979), and enable the child to understand that people may not always show what they are feeling. Children who have mastered display rules may not take facial expressions at 'face value' but instead modify their judgements of emotions in others in accordance with contextual cues (Reichenbach and Masters, 1983). As display rules represent social conventions that are only gradually understood by children (Saarni, 1979), some indication of appreciation of such conventions by children with LD would indicate a development of social sensitivity similar to that of non-LD children.

As pointed out earlier, children with LD have been found to be less proficient on identifying expressions of emotions. However, increased accuracy with age among children with LD has been observed, suggesting that the skills required on these tasks are developmental in nature, even for children with LD. In one study, the relative use of expressive and situational cues in judgements of emotions by children with LD was examined and compared with that of non-LD children (Nabuzoka, 1993). Two groups of children with LD, a younger group (mean 8.6 years) and an older group (11 years) were compared with a group of non-LD children matched for mental age with the older group of children with LD. The children were shown video episodes of actors facially expressing emotions on their own, in neutral situations, in situations consistent with the expressed emotion, in situations conflicting with the expressed emotion, and in situations without any visibly expressed emotion. The task was to identify an emotional label as characteristic of each episode from those supplied by the experimenter, and to give an explanation for the choice.

The result was that non-LD children performed better than children with LD. The former also identified emotions evoked by given situations in the absence of facial expressions to a greater extent than children with LD. In addition, non-LD children used more situational than expressive cues where the two types of cue were consistent, and used the situational cues to a greater extent overall than children with LD. Where situational and expressive cues conflicted, younger children with LD used expressive cues to a greater extent than older children with LD and also to a greater extent than non-LD children. The younger children with LD also relied more on expressive cues than situational cues overall.

These findings again suggest developmental differentiation

between children with LD and other children, and between younger and older children with LD. Non-LD children, while being generally more adept at identifying emotional cues, rely less on expressive and more on situational cues. Such differentiation may be more evident where expressive and situational cues conflict. Though no age/disability group effects were found for relying on situational cues or both situational and expressive cues, the younger group of children with LD relied on expressive cues to a significantly greater extent than both the older group of children with LD and non-LD children. The younger children with LD also cited expressive cues more frequently than situational cues.

It has been suggested that less preference for expressive cues and more for situational cues may indicate developmental maturity, supporting the hypothesis that developmentally older children are more aware of social display rules and thus rely less on expressions as they may mask an individual's true feelings (Saarni, 1979; Gnepp and Hess, 1986). Thus, the performance of non-LD children would indicate more advanced social cognitive development, while some developmental progression also exists amongst children with LD. This is consistent with findings in studies on non-LD children. In such studies, and where expressive and situational cues were discrepant, younger children preferred expressive cues while older children preferred situational or contextual cues (Gnepp, 1983; Hoffner and Badzinski, 1989; Reichenbach and Masters, 1983; Wiggers and van Lieshout, 1985).

Wiggers and van Lieshout (1985) suggested that reliance on situational or expressive cues, when there was a discrepancy between cues, did not reflect a preference for either type of cue, but rather for cues depicting the most recognizable emotion, such as those of simple in preference to complex ones and for emotional cues in preference to neutral ones. The children in Wiggers and van Lieshout's study were observed to rely more on situational cues when both types of cues depicted simple emotions, a reliance that became more pronounced with age, and only when labels were supplied. In Nabuzoka's (1993) study involving children with LD, both types of cue depicted simple emotions including happiness, fear, sadness, anger, disgust, and surprise. Where neutral expressions or situations were depicted they were not the designated cues, and in all cases labels were given. On the basis of Wiggers and Van Lieshout's observations, one would expect the children to rely on situational cues to a larger extent than expressive cues. However, not all children relied more on the situational cues. Instead, the younger children with LD significantly relied more on expressive cues than on situational ones. The performance by older children with LD, though to a lesser extent and not statistically significant, also pointed in the same direction. Only non-LD children did show greater reliance on situational cues than expressive cues where the types of cues were consistent with one another.

There are also some indications that reliance on one type of cue across age/disability status may involve more than a mere shift from noticing only one type of cue to considering both types of cue. Nabu-zoka observed that even the younger children with LD noticed both situational and expressive cues even though they relied more on expressive ones, a finding consistent with studies on typically developing children (Gnepp, 1983; Hoffner and Badzinski, 1989). For example, mere references to both types of cue did not increase as a function of age or disability status. Instead, younger children with LD referred to both cues as frequently as older children with LD, while non-LD children referred to both cues less frequently. On the other hand, when asked to explain their choice of emotion, non-LD children resolved the conflicting situational and expressive cues to a greater extent than either group of children with LD. This involved offering an explanation for the presence of both cues. For example, one task involves an episode of conflicting situational and expressive cues where a mother is presented as being fearful of mice (fear being the contextual cue), but has an angry expression on her face (anger being the conflicting expressive cue). In trying to explain the existence of an angry expression on her face when a son presented her with a mouse (i.e. a fear-inducing situation), the children would explain that she was probably angry at the son for showing it to her when he *knew* she feared mice. Such reconstruction of the situation or meaning of facial expressions has been observed for developmentally older children in other studies (Gnepp, 1983).

The fact that children with LD resolved fewer conflicting cues suggests impaired social cognitive development. Resolution of conflicting cues, and preference for situational rather than expressive cues, both point to greater social cognitive ability. They involve not only the perception of available cues, but also their interpretation and weighing-up. In the episode involving a mother and the mouse, for example, non-LD children and, to a lesser extent, older children with LD indicated that the mother was in fact afraid. That involves social information processing by the child (see Chapter 4).

Less developmentally advanced children may, however, be influenced more by the salience of one type of cue when considering conflicting cues (Wiggers and van Lieshout, 1985). It has been suggested that, for younger children, facial cues may be especially salient (Hoffner and Badzinski, 1989; Reichenbach and Masters, 1983). This is because, from infancy, children associate facial expressions with common emotions such as happy and sad and are responsive to affective meaning of the expressions (Campos *et al.*, 1983). Thus, reliance on expressive cues may not make much cognitive demand on the child, as an emotion such as 'happiness' would tend to be directly linked with the expression. Developmentally younger children would thus recog-

nize the expressed emotion much more easily as they only have to consider the target individual's manifest attributes.

Situational cues, in contrast, require one to link a multitude of related information. Where the social cues are congruent, identifying the
correct emotion may not be too demanding. In such conditions, it can
indeed be argued that the availability of both situational and expressive cues may even amplify the meaning of the cues present, thereby
making it easier for both younger and older children with LD. Such a
view would be consistent with the findings of Wiggers and van
Lieshout (1985): when situational and expressive cues were represen-
tative of one particular emotion, the majority of girls aged between 4
and 10 years were able to recognize the emotion.

There is some evidence, however, that expressive and situational
cues may not be simply additive when information is consistent.
Reichenbach and Masters (1983) found that, while consistent contextual and expressive information allowed more accurate judgements than
expressive cues alone, it did not lead to more accurate recognition of
emotional states than contextual information alone. This suggests that
a complex process is involved in children understanding situational
determinants of affective states. For educators, this has implications for
social-skills training of children with LD. It means, for example, that
mere pairing of expressive cues with emotive situations may not be
adequate. On the other hand, more emphasis on social display rules
may better prepare these children to interpret social situations accurately.

Another consideration is possible gender differences in children's
understanding of affective states. Nabuzoka (1993) found that girls
overall identified situational cues with neutral expressions to a greater
extent than boys. When situational and expressive cues conflicted,
gender differences were observed regarding reliance on situational
cues for non-LD children but not for children with LD. In this situation,
non-LD girls used situational cues to a greater extent than boys. There
was some developmental differentiation amongst girls with LD, however. Older girls with LD used more situational cues than younger girls
with LD, while non-LD girls relied more on situational cues than both
groups of girls with LD. Amongst boys, older children with LD used
situational cues to a greater extent than both younger children with LD
and non-LD children. These findings suggest that the effects of gender
on social sensitivity may be different for children with LD and non-LD
children. In addition – and if greater reliance on situational than
expressive cues represents more cognitive advancement – the findings
suggest that girls tend to be developmentally more advanced than
boys on this aspect of social perception.

Conclusion

For children with LD, there is a developmental progression towards less reliance on expressive cues of emotion and more on situational ones. This is similar to what is found with non-LD children. However, while it indicates that children with LD may not necessarily follow a different course, they nonetheless tend to be developmentally less advanced. There are also some indications of gender differences. Girls with LD appear to be more advanced than boys of similar chronological age.

The shift from reliance on expressive to situational or contextual cues suggests social cognitive advancement, as it implies interpretation and making inferences. There are some indications, from research on non-LD children, that complex cognitive processes are involved in the use of both types of cue in social situations. Those processes include an appreciation of social display rules, and that has implications for social-skills training of children with LD.

Abilities that are related to social perceptual skills, but which reflect a spectrum of social cognitive skills, include social perspective-taking and empathic skills. In the light of the observed developmental trend towards preference for situational cues, and the cognitive implications of such a shift, an interesting question is whether similar patterns of functioning obtain in those domains. The next section addresses that question.

Social inference and role-taking abilities

Some studies have shown that children with LD tend to 'misread' social situations overall (e.g. Bruno, 1981; Gerber and Zinkgraf, 1982; Stiladis and Wiener, 1989), and that they are also less adept at making inferences based on subtle emotional and social situations (Pearl and Cosden, 1982). Developmental patterns have also been observed on these abilities. In one study, Gerber and Zinkgraf (1982) individually administered the Test of Social Inference (TSI; Edmonson *et al.*, 1974) to two groups of children with LD, aged 7–8 and 10–11 years respectively, and two groups of non-LD children of like ages. The TSI requires subjects to give interpretations of 30 pictures showing various situations. Subjects with high social inferential ability are believed to be able to infer multiple social dimensions from each picture, to make full sense of the situations, and to respond to them in appropriate fashions. Responses are scored according to the level of overall comprehension demonstrated and the degree to which the response is complete and unambiguous. Edmonson and colleagues reported that children with LD did not perform as well as non-LD peers, and that older children tended to score higher than did younger ones. Comparison of the performance of older children with

LD with that of younger non-LD children did not show any significant difference.

The importance of these findings is that, not only did children with LD lack the social decoding abilities of non-LD peers, but also these skills appeared to be developmental in nature, and children with LD apparently lagged behind their non-LD peer group, as opposed to being deficient in social functioning *per se* (which would have been indicated had older children with LD not performed better than younger ones). Another interesting finding was that older children with LD did not differ significantly from younger non-LD children on the experimental task. Taken together, these two findings suggest that children with LD could develop the skills measured by the experiment, but they probably understood the social environment only as well as non-LD peers who were 2–4 years younger (Gerber and Zinkgraf, 1982).

Other studies have looked at the children's role-taking abilities and comprehension of non-verbal communication. Role-taking skills generally refer to a child's ability to adopt the perspective of another person, to infer his or her thoughts and feelings. Though studies comparing children's role-taking skills with their social behaviours and peer acceptance have neither confirmed nor refuted their importance for successful interpersonal functioning, several investigators have compared children with LD and non-LD children on such skills. The results have been equivocal, with some reporting negative results and others reporting mixed or positive findings.

A review by LaGreca (1981) indicated that, when males with LD were compared with non-LD males of comparable intelligence quotient (IQ), and standard role-taking tasks were employed, no differences between the two groups were apparent. Poor role-taking skills were thus not implicated as problematic for males with LD in this study. However, it was pointed out that the nature of role-taking deficits in females needed to be examined systematically. In addition, IQ and age, and the specific type of disability displayed by the child, appeared to be factors confounding the findings. It was also suggested that studies needed to relate role-taking skills to actual social behaviours and measures of peer acceptance so as to establish a link between social cognitive abilities and peer relationships for children with LD. Furthermore, there were suggestions of possible subgroup differences within the population of individuals with LD (Wiener, 1980).

Wiener (1980) related subtypes of learning disabilities to different kinds of peer and interpersonal difficulties. Children with spatial difficulties were viewed as most likely to experience problems in interpreting non-verbal social cues. These children have also been described as having poor body image and difficulties with visual discrimination (Wiig and Harris, 1974). More recently, Rourke (1989) posited two primary types of learning disabilities: the non-verbal LD syndrome and the verbal (phonological) LD syndrome. He proposed that those with non-verbal LD have poor overall social adaptation owing to social problem-solving deficits and difficulties with identifying and understanding facial expressions and non-verbal communications, whereas those with verbal LD may not have these particular problems.

The hypothesis that subgroups of children with LD may have different kinds of peer and interpersonal difficulties still requires empirical verification. However, a number of studies have been concerned with comparing children with specific type of disability on their sensitivity to non-verbal cues. The social perceptual abilities of subgroups of children with LD, based on whether they have verbal or non-verbal deficits, have been found to differ. For example, children with verbal deficits have been found to perform better than those with non-verbal deficits on identification of facial expressions of affect (Dimitrovsky *et al.*, 1998). However, non-LD children tend to perform better, overall, than children with LD. Of particular interest from a practical perspective are the ways in which such subgroup differences could be related to the children's social behaviour, and the resultant implications for their social adjustment.

Social functioning of children with social perception difficulties

Introduction
Studies considered so far indicate that children with LD perform relatively poorly on perception and interpretation of emotions. They also perform worse in skills involving empathy, role-taking and making social inferences. Such findings are often interpreted as indicating that children with LD have difficulties in the general social perceptual domain. They suggest that the children may be impaired in the ability to perceive social cues.

However, the concept of 'social perception', when used in this context, seems to be over-generalized to include a much more complex construct involving social cognitive attributes. The latter may be one of the underlying factors that could explain the apparent impaired social adjustment of children with LD. For example, social perception as used in this context simply refers to one's ability to gather information from a total social field including expressive and contextual cues. The information so gathered, however, needs to be processed in terms of relative importance, and a direction for social action often needs to be formulated on that basis to enable the individual to meet the demands of the situation. The latter two aspects of social functioning involve making social inferences from available cues, and are essentially cognitive skills going beyond mere social perception. Such skills are also much more directly related to social adjustment. Specifically, the resultant social action that one formulates reflects adaptive behavioural skills likely to set the tone for the quality of social relations.

Unsatisfactory social relations of children with LD should thus reflect limitations in their socio-adaptive skills. These limitations could in turn result from problems with any one or a combination of the following: identifying relevant social cues, processing of the social cues, formulation of a direction for social action, and the actual behavioural skills possessed. These represent a spectrum of social functioning of which social perception is one part that could be considered as a precursor of social cognition. Social cognitive skills of children with LD as reflected in information processing and formulation of responses are discussed more extensively in Chapter 4. Given that children with LD have difficulties in identifying social cues, the task for researchers is to determine whether and/or how these difficulties might be related to behaviour as an aspect of social functioning (see Chapter 5). Of specific concern is how the behaviour of children with LD reflects difficulties in decoding social cues.

Social perception and behaviour

One view is that a reduced ability to recognize social cues may reflect a difference in general perceptual or cognitive development of children with LD (Johnson and Myklebust, 1967; Wiig and Harris, 1974). Generally, there has been an apparent low-to-moderate relationship between performance on social cognitive tasks and children's level of intelligence (Chandler, 1977; Shantz, 1983), but studies examining such links have been rather scarce (Gray *et al.*, 1983). One particular problem with studies that were initially carried out under this framework was an inability to distinguish object and person perception, and their implications for social functioning. For example, a number of studies compared role-taking skills of children with LD and non-LD peers without establishing empirically the importance of such skills for successful interpersonal functioning (LaGreca, 1981). Such conceptual problems make it difficult to establish the nature of a relationship between the various domains of children's functioning. These and other methodological difficulties are discussed at length in Chapter 7. The point here is that any link between perceptual skills and social behaviour should reflect the former as relevant to functioning in the social domain.

Other researchers have explained the performance of children with LD on social perceptual tasks in terms of a social developmental lag (Gerber and Zinkgraf, 1982; Jackson *et al.*, 1987; Nabuzoka and Smith, 1995). This has been supported by research where performance by children with LD has been observed to improve with age. However, such improvement does not mean that children with LD catch up with non-LD peers, as the latter have been observed to perform better than chronologically older children with LD matched for mental age. In addition, the ability to recognize social cues at certain age levels may vary depending on the type and mode of expression of cues (Nabuzoka and Smith, 1995). Patterns of social perception that are similar to those of non-LD children, but characterized by developmental delays, have implications for the behaviour of children with LD.

Differences between children with LD and non-LD peers in the quality, and not the type, of behaviours exhibited may explain social difficulties of children with LD who do not show significant behavioural problems. There are some indications that children with LD may tend to be viewed as less desirable as friends even when they do not often engage in aggressive, disruptive or otherwise overtly negative behaviour (Nabuzoka and Smith, 1993; see also Chapter 5). Differences between children with LD and non-LD peers in behavioural attributes that apparently explain such maladjustment are much more subtle, but suggest that such children are perceptually and cognitively less socially competent. For example, children with LD have been found to be generally less responsive during interpersonal interactions (Mathinos, 1991). Such limited responsiveness suggests failure to detect social interaction cues or prompts (Sisterhen and Gerber, 1989).

In terms of communicative behaviour, it has been observed that conversations of children with LD tend to be less appropriate in situations with ambiguous cues, but not in structured situations with less ambiguous cues (Pearl *et al.*, 1986). Ambiguous situations involve conflicting cues that require resolving and are therefore likely to be more cognitively demanding. As we saw earlier, the ability to resolve conflicting cues and to rely on contextual ones has been found to reflect developmental progression in children with LD. However, the developmental lag of these children suggests differences in social cognitive functioning.

Summary and conclusions

Research indicates that children with LD tend to be less accurate in perception of social cues than other children of similar chronological age. Their social perceptual skills do improve with time, without reaching the level of their non-LD peers. This suggests that while children with LD may be less effective than non-LD children in this domain of social functioning, the limitations may be more quantitative than qualitative.

It could be said that since social perceptual skills include the ability to decode cues, qualitative limitations in the functioning of children with LD might not be very apparent in this domain. Such limitations may, however, manifest themselves in the analysis or processing of such cues, and in social interaction. Thus, what may be quantitative differences in the social perceptual domain may be reflected in qualitative differences in behaviour.

This has implications for training children with LD in relevant social perceptual and cognitive skills. For example, one possible area of focus for trainers could be an emphasis on situational determinants of people's affective states and the development of an appreciation of social conventions such as display rules.

Difficulties in social perception are likely to be associated with lack of adaptability and may be manifested in poor judgement and problems in interpersonal relations. Some of the empirical basis for a linkage between social perceptual limitations of children with LD and their social behaviour are discussed further in Chapter 6. Of particular concern is whether these behaviours necessarily and without qualification precipitate interpersonal problems. There is also a need to identify the mechanisms by which social perceptual abilities may be linked to behavioural outcomes. One such mechanism is social information processing as an aspect of social cognitive functioning. This is discussed extensively in the next chapter.

Chapter 4

Social cognitive functioning

It was suggested in the last chapter that children with learning dificulties (LD) tend to be less adept at perception of social cues than do non-LD children of similar age, but their limitations appear to be more quantitative than qualitative. Since most tasks on social perception include identification or recognition of cues, comparisons between children with LD and others have focused on the range of cues that can be decoded. In this respect, qualitative limitations in the functioning of children with LD may not be apparent in this domain. These limitations may, however, manifest themselves in the analysis or processing of such cues in the context of social interaction. Such differentiation has been indicated where the children require to take into consideration both situational and expressive cues, especially where these may be conflicting.

Consideration of both types of cue, and arriving at a decision as to which should carry the most weight, requires much more than social perceptual skills. It requires *identification* of which available cues are relevant, correctly *interpreting* what they mean, and making an *evaluation* of their relevance to the situation. The latter is obviously a function of social experience. One thus requires an ability to *process* the social information presented in a given situation before reaching a decision about what it all means for the participants. Children who more accurately recognize the situational determinants of an individual's affective state will be those with greater ability at social information processing.

Social information processing can be considered to be one aspect of social competence, facilitating appropriate behaviour and thereby eliciting the positive regard of others (Dodge *et al.*, 1986; McFall, 1982). Development from a sole reliance on expressive cues to include situational ones reflects greater social awareness and a growth in social competence. In most cases 'social competence' is used to refer to an individual's characteristic way of behaving in social situations, as well as the efficacy of their behaviour. However, a large measure of what we call 'socially competent behaviour' reflects one's skills in social understanding. This chapter is concerned with the latter domain of functioning.

Childhood social information processing

The processing of social information by a child is central to his or her understanding of the world. This involves extracting meaning from a wide range of cues and sources of information, such as the nature of the social situation, speech, body postures and facial expressions. It includes using the analysis of meaning to make inferences about others' thoughts and feelings, and to generate ideas about their inner state. Children with problems in processing social information generally have difficulty understanding and adjusting to their social world.

It was shown in earlier chapters that some children with LD do not function effectively in social interactions and that they experience more adjustment problems than do non-LD peers. If interpersonal functioning and adjustment is related to social information processing, one would expect children with LD to have difficulties in social information processing. The initial task, therefore, is to establish the extent and nature of these difficulties. The next task is to determine whether any problems that children with LD have in the social cognitive domain can explain their difficulties in social relations.

While a number of studies have examined the social information processing skills of non-LD children, there have been few on children with LD. The studies have been based on the social information processing (SIP) model proposed by Dodge and colleagues (Crick and Dodge, 1994; Dodge *et al.*, 1986). They suggest some link between social information processing and social adjustment (Harrist *et al.*, 1997). Some of those studies relevant to functioning of children with LD will be examined in this chapter. First the SIP model will be outlined.

A social cognitive model

According to the SIP framework, a typically developing child's behavioural response in a social situation follows a set of sequential information processing steps. The five-step model was explained in Chapter 1 (see page 20). According to the model, deficiencies in processing occur either when the child fails to consider a step, or when the child responds in an inaccurate or biased manner at a particular step. Such deficiencies are reflected in the child's behavioural enactment and peers' judgements. Thus, poor SIP has been linked to poor peer relationships and other indices of maladjustment (Dodge and Frame, 1982; Murphy *et al.*, 1992; Quiggle *et al.*, 1992; for a review, see Crick and Dodge, 1994).

Dodge and his colleagues examined this aspect of social cognitive functioning by focusing on the relationship between social information processing and behaviour (Dodge *et al.*, 1986). Socially competent and incompetent (based on teacher and peer ratings) kindergarten through second-grade children (pre-school age to about 7 years of age) were presented with videotaped stimuli designed to assess patterns of processing information about possible entry to a peer group. In another session, children were asked to participate in an actual group entry task with two peers from their classroom. Measures of each of the five steps of processing were found to predict children's competence and success at this behavioural task, with increments in prediction being provided by several steps of processing. A child's performance at peer group entry significantly predicted peers' judgements of him or her, and those judgements in turn significantly predicted the peers' behaviour toward that child.

The research by Dodge and his colleagues has important implications for social functioning and adjustment of children with LD. In addition to illustrating the relationship between two indices of social competence commonly examined in previous studies (i.e. patterns of social behaviour and judgements by others), the findings are interesting in various other respects.

First, the study further illuminated the relationship between others' judgements of the child and their behaviour towards that child. In the light of these findings one would interpret patterns of social interaction observed in studies of heterogeneous groups of children with LD and non-LD children to reflect this relationship. Thus the preference by non-LD children to interact frequently with other non-LD peers could indicate some sort of negative judgement of children with LD by their non-LD peers. Such judgements would be based on previously observed social behaviour of the children with LD (see Chapter 5 for further discussion of this relationship). In this respect, preference by non-LD peers to interact with other non-LD peers and not children with LD could reflect a lack of social competence on the part of the latter children.

The second important finding of the study by Dodge and his colleagues is the relationship between social cognitive abilities and behavioural competence in social relations. An individual's behaviour is more often in response to environmental stimulation or cues. While the stimulus for much of the behaviour of adults may at most times not be perceptible in the immediate surroundings, children's play behaviour tends to be influenced by the immediate surroundings. What happens between a child's perception of a given social situation and that child's enactment of an act or response has a lot to do with his or her social cognitive abilities. According to the information processing model, a child's level of social competence will to some extent be determined by that child's ability to process social information through the various interrelated but discrete steps.

Implicitly, a child who has difficulties in social relations would, according to this model, have difficulties in *processing* social information. In the view of Dodge and coworkers:

> '*Skilful processing requires consideration of each step. Deficiencies in processing occur either when the child fails to consider a step (such as when a child enacts a generalised response without evaluating its potential consequences) or when the child responds in an inaccurate or biased manner at a particular step (such as when a child misinterprets a peer's cues).*'

> (Dodge *et al.*, 1986, p. 5)

Thus, problems experienced by children with LD in peer relations may emanate from deficits in their processing of environmental cues. The relationship between social cognitive abilities, behaviour and social adjustment is represented in the model depicted in Figure 1.2 (see Chapter 1). On this basis, the nature of problems faced by children with LD in their social functioning may be such that, for a given child, the problem lies in one or more of these domains. It could also manifest itself differently at different age levels or in different contexts. Studies on perception of emotions (Hobson, 1986a, b; Holder and Kirkpatrick, 1991; Nabuzoka and Smith, 1995) and other social cues, and also those on the ability to impute mental states to others or attribution of knowledge and beliefs (Baron-Cohen *et al.*, 1985), suggest that learning disabilities can be associated with specific problems in dealing with social information (Clements, 1987). Assessment of the children's performance on tasks designed to represent specific steps from the onset of social stimuli to a behavioural response enables the identification of the specific levels of difficulties in either the perception and/or processing of social information.

Specific studies on social information processing

Given that errors in social information processing are hypothesized to lead to inappropriate or undesirable behaviour, a link first needs to be established between these children's social cognitive functioning and their behaviour. Then, if difficulties in social relations reflect inappropriate or undesirable behaviour, the social cognitive basis of such behaviour can be addressed. According to the SIP model, one might identify the level at which a problem arises. For example, (a) attending to and (b) interpretation of social cues such as emotional expressions represent successive steps in information processing, and failure to perceive the emotional expressions would indicate that the problem is at the attentional level. Alternatively, the problem might be further on in the processing system, such that though the children may *notice* social cues, they may have difficulties in interpreting them.

A number of studies have shown that children with LD and non-LD classmates differ on measures of each of the five steps of the SIP model. For example:

- Studies of encoding have found that children with LD do worse in their comprehension of social cues (Bryan, 1977).
- With regard to mental representation and interpretation, students with LD have been found to be less competent at understanding the intentions of others (Weiss, 1984; Nabuzoka and Smith, 1999).
- In studies examining response search, boys with LD have shown fewer skills in developing goals and strategies (Oliva and LaGreca, 1988), and they have been found to be less skilful in choosing strategies to resolve social situations (Carlson, 1987).
- Students with LD have also been found to perform worse in generating solutions to social problems (Toro *et al.*, 1990).
- Differences between students with LD and non-LD students have also been found on response decisions to situations (Bryan *et al.*, 1982).
- Finally, students with LD have been found to be less tactful and less persuasive than their classmates in behavioural enactment (Bryan *et al.*, 1981a).

These studies suggest that children with LD are generally less effective at social information processing. However, the information provided by such studies regarding the social cognitive skills of children with LD has been fragmented. This is because they have mostly assessed one or two of the SIP steps. Very few have examined the social cognitive skills of children with LD at each of the steps of the SIP model.

Nabuzoka (1993) reported one such study. Two groups of children with LD (average ages 9 and 11 years) and a comparative group of non-LD children (average 9 years) were assessed. Two video stimulus tapes were prepared with the assistance of child actors. The tapes were similar in all respects, with the exception that the actors differed (one tape with each gender) so that subjects could view a set of stimuli about peers of their own gender. The video scenes included episodes where the child actors were at play displaying some facial and verbal cues.

In the first scene on each tape, two children were seated at a table, playing a board game. Each took several turns before the scene ended. During the scene, one of the children was visibly enjoying himself/herself (had a happy facial expression) and the other looked thoughtful and somewhat unsatisfied or bored. A third child was alone a few metres away, playing with some toys. 'We need another player,' says the second child, looking towards the third. 'No, I rather like it with only the two of us,' says the first child, smilingly. 'We only need more toys to play with. Why don't we get some?'

Specific cues presented in this scene included the following: (a) facial expressions – happy versus thoughtful, unsatisfied; (b) verbal expressions – 'need another player' versus 'no, ... like it with only the two of us'; and (c) gesture – look towards the third child (invitingly?). The third child then approached the two children but the scene ended just before the actor attempted anything.

The next episode consisted of the original scene of two children playing a game followed by the arrival of the third child who attempted to join the two children at play. The entry child then displayed five strategies in turn: a polite request to join in ('competent'); barging into a game ('aggressive'); citing own competence, for example: 'I can do that ...' ('self-centred'); hovering behaviour ('passive-shy'); and a reference to right to play, for example: 'The teacher said I should play ...' ('authority intervention'). Each scene ended just before the host children could respond.

The participants were assessed as to:

- whether they identified the cues presented (step 1 – encoding);
- their interpretation of presented cues (step 2);
- the range of possible strategies for joining the play scene, before viewing the enacted strategies (step 3 – response search);
- whether or not they endorsed depicted group entry behaviour (step 4 – evaluation);
- self description and role-play of their own group entry behaviour (step 5 – enactment).

The results showed differences between the groups of children according to age and disability status. These developmental effects were observed for four of the five social information processing steps representing cue utilization (1), accessing of potential responses (3), response evaluation (4), and enactment (5). Only the step involving mental representation or interpretation of social cues (2) did not show any developmental differences. At all these stages, non-LD children performed better than either group of children with LD, and older children with LD performed better than younger ones, except for the step involving accessing of potential responses (response search). At this stage, non-LD children generated more solutions than did children with LD, but younger children with LD generated more potential solutions than did older children with LD. However, examination of the proportion of competent responses generated suggested a finding confirming that the general trend related to age/disability. This showed that while developmentally less advanced children generated as many potential solutions as did non-LD children, a larger proportion of such solutions were less likely to be appropriate to the situation than those generated by developmentally advanced children. These findings are presented in Table 4.1.

Comparisons of correlation between the composite variables representing the processing steps showed a pattern for children with LD generally similar to that of non-LD children, but with some specific differences. Encoding (cue utilization) was significantly correlated with appropriate self-description of entry behaviour (enactment) for children with LD but not for non-LD children. For children with LD,

Table 4.1 *Mean scores on social information processing steps for children with and without LD (Nabuzoka, 1993)*

Measure label (processing step)	Age/disability			Effects	
	Younger (LD) (*n* = 25)	Older (LD) (*n* = 20)	Non-LD (*n* = 25)	*F*	*p*
ENCODING (step 1)	0.64	1.10	1.64	4.44	0.02
Present cues	0.48	0.55	1.24	6.02	0.004
Inferred cues	0.16	0.55	0.52	1.98	ns
Absent/irrelevant cues	0.92	0.80	0.72	0.09	ns
INTERPRETATION (step 2)	1.88	1.87	1.90	.042	ns
SOLUTIONS GENERATED (step 3)	1.76	1.65	3.00	7.08	0.002
Proportion of competent responses	0.64	0.80	1.72	12.08	0.0001
Proportion of aggressive responses	0.84	0.25	0.56	1.80	ns
ACCURACY OF RESPONSE EVALUATION (step 4)	1.08	1.30	1.64	3.14	0.05
Endorsement of competent responses	4.48	5.05	4.96	0.58	ns
Endorsement of aggressive responses	2.68	2.30	2.08	2.25	ns
Endorsement of self-centred responses	3.76	2.95	3.04	1.30	ns
Endorsement of passive responses	3.12	3.60	3.56	1.00	ns
Endorsement of authority intervention responses	3.20	2.60	3.00	0.53	ns
ENACTMENT (step 5)	1.88	2.35	2.84	5.14	.01

response search, measured by the total number of solutions generated for the peer group entry situation, was significantly correlated with the proportion of competent solutions generated, accuracy of response evaluation and appropriateness of self-descriptive entry behaviour. The proportion of competent solutions was significantly correlated with response evaluation and self-description of entry behaviour for children with LD but not for non-LD children. For non-LD children, the total number of solutions generated was significantly correlated only with the proportion of competent solutions. Response evaluation was significantly correlated with self-description of appropriate entry behaviour for both children with LD and non-LD children.

In all, Nabuzoka (1993) found that children with LD who encoded relevant social cues also reported more appropriate self-behavioural enactment of group entry. In addition, performance at any one of the processing steps of response search, response evaluation, and enactment could predict performance at any of the other steps. For non-LD children, two parallel relationships were observed: potential group entry solutions generated were more often competent ones; and those who made accurate evaluation of responses and selected optimal choices also reported more appropriate self-entry behaviour (enactment). For children with LD, encoding included identification and use of available social cues as well as those that could be inferred from the situation. Children who encoded relevant cues made less use of irrelevant cues but generated more self-centred solutions. Non-LD children who scored highly at encoding, like children with LD, also used more social cues available and made greater use of inferred cues. In addition, those making more accurate cue interpretation made less use of irrelevant cues. Response search, for children with LD, consisted of the ability to generate competent solutions, passive solutions, as well as aggressive solutions. Children identifying more cues available generated more potential entry behaviours, and endorsed polite requests to join peers to a greater extent. For non-LD children, generating potential entry behaviours was likely to include competent as well as aggressive solutions, as with children with LD. But unlike children with LD, they were also likely to generate authority-based solutions. Children with LD identifying and using available cues also generated competent solutions to the peer group entry situation, and accurately evaluated the efficacy and consequences of responses.

In general terms, significant age/disability effects indicate that older children with LD are more advanced at social information processing than younger ones, but may still be developmentally delayed relative to chronologically same-age non-LD children. These findings are consistent with those on social perception (see Chapter 3) and point to social cognitive delays in children with LD. One finding in particular relates to performance on interpretation of presented cues (step 2) and response search (step 3) (see Table 4.1). On these steps, younger children with LD apparently outperform older children. In the latter case, the significance of the difference in performance on the processing step of response search may lie not so much in the actual number of solutions as the type of solutions generated. The proportion of competent responses was, for example, low for younger children with LD, higher for older children, and highest for non-LD children. This is consistent with developmental differences. It suggests that while non-LD children may have a greater capacity for generating potential solutions to situational tasks, the developmental significance of the differences in solutions generated may be in the *quality* of the solutions, other than sheer *quantity*, thus indicating more cognitive differentiation (Rubin and Krasnor, 1986).

Nabuzoka's finding on cue interpretation (step 2) indicates a lack of developmental differentiation at this step, which may in fact be due to the construct validity of the measure. Children were asked to indicate whether the host children would allow a third child to join them. A high score represented a perception of positive inclination by the child, and a child indicating a negative inclination got a lower score. In this respect a child indicating a negative inclination, but on the basis of inferred cues, would get a low score despite having reached what could have been a logical conclusion. Linking the score with an explanation for the children's interpretation (used in this case to score for cue utilization, step 1) may be a more accurate measure. Other studies have used some standard criteria for accuracy of interpretation and found developmental differentiation (Gomez and Hazeldine, 1996; Nabuzoka and Smith, 1999).

Gomez and Hazeldine used the SIP model of Dodge and colleagues to compare the social information processing skills of children with LD (defined as 'mild mentally retarded') and two non-LD groups: one matched for chronological age (CA) and another for mental age (MA). They used six sets of drawn pictures depicting provocation by a peer, directed towards either a child or the child's play objects. Two of the sets of drawings showed the peer being deliberately hostile, two showed unintentional accidents, and two were ambiguous as to the intention of the peer. After presentation of each set of drawings, the children in the study were asked questions about the intention of the peer. This was so as to elicit measures of accuracy of interpretation to accidental and hostile cues, and attribution of ambiguous cues (assessing step 2 of Dodge's SIP model). The children were also asked how they would respond if they were the victim in the drawings, and responses were scored for being hostile or non-hostile to all three types of cues (assessing response generation, or step 3 of the model).

The children with LD were found to be less accurate than the CA-matched non-LD group for total accuracy across cues and accuracy of interpretation of accidental scenarios. There were no differences on these measures between the non-LD groups, nor between the children with LD and the MA-matched non-LD group. In addition, children with LD significantly generated more hostile behavioural responses than did CA-matched non-LD children on all sets of scenarios taken together, but no significant differences were observed between children with LD and the MA-matched group, nor between the non-LD groups. The children with LD also generated significantly more hostile responses to the ambiguous cues than did both the CA- and the MA-matched groups, while no significant differences were observed between the non-LD groups. There were no significant differences between children with LD and the MA-matched group in behavioural responses to accidental stimuli, but both groups generated more hostile behavioural responses than did the CA-matched group.

These findings by Gomez and Hazeldine thus show an overall trend towards more differences between children with LD and CA-matched children than between children with LD and MA-matched children. However, when aggression and hyperactivity ratings were partialed out, fewer differences were obtained between children with LD and the non-LD groups: children with LD indicated more hostile behaviour responses than MA-matched children only to the ambiguous cues. This would seem to suggest that the presence of these behaviour problems (i.e. hyperactivity and aggression) affect the SIP skills of children with LD. In addition, the findings indicate that children with LD are more hostile than non-LD children, matched for both CA and MA, in response generation (step 3 of Dodge's SIP model) when required to process ambiguous social cues, but not for clearly hostile or accidental cues. Gomez and Hazeldine suggested that ambiguous cues may require cognitive abilities beyond those possessed by children with LD, and that when presented with difficulties in interpreting social cues, children with LD are thus more likely than non-LD children to respond in a hostile manner.

Difficulties in interpreting social cues that may be ambiguous or conflicting are likely to manifest themselves in social problem-solving tasks. Studies on children with LD generally suggest that such children have poorer social cognitive problem-solving skills than do non-LD peers. Children with LD have been reported to offer fewer and less varied problem-solving strategies than non-LD children matched for chronological age, and have difficulties adapting appropriate cognitive strategies to social situations (Gerber, 1983). However, they do not differ from non-LD children matched for mental age (Smith, 1986).

One social problem-solving task involving ambiguous cues and being particularly problematic for children with LD is the need to distinguish serious fighting and playful (rough-and-tumble) fighting. The latter is play that may superficially appear aggressive, and thus be confused with serious fighting, because it involves wrestling, grappling, hitting, kicking, restraining, chasing, and fleeing. All this occurs in a playful mode; but because it appears similar to serious fighting, a child with social cognitive difficulties may not interpret a play initiation correctly and respond as if it were hostile. Such difficulties have been observed with non-LD children with problems in social relations (Dodge and Frame, 1982; Pellegrini, 1988). It has been suggested that children with LD may have similar problems and be less accurate than non-LD children in distinguishing initiations of rough-and-tumble play from serious fighting (Nabuzoka and Smith, 1999). Social cognitive difficulties of this nature may underline difficulties of children with LD in social relations as they are frequently likely to lead to inappropriate responses.

Nabuzoka and Smith (1999) studied two groups of children with LD: a younger group with an average age of 9.3 years and an older group with an average of 11.8 years. A third group consisted of non-LD children matched on MA with the older group of children with LD. These groups of children were compared on abilities to distinguish rough-and-tumble from serious fighting. The children were shown video episodes of children of about the same age range and asked to make a judgement as to whether each episode was play or serious fighting. About half the episodes were rough-and-tumble and the others were actual fighting. The children were also required to give reasons (criteria) for their judgements. The two groups of children with LD were found to be less accurate in making the distinction. In addition, children with LD used a smaller range of criteria in making the distinction; used some criteria less than others; and were much more unlikely to give any reason for judgements made (see Figure 4.1). However, the order in frequency of those criteria cited was similar for both non-LD children and children with LD, and older children with LD were more accurate than younger children in making the distinction.

These findings indicate that children with LD use fewer social cues and are less accurate in interpreting the nature of behavioural episodes. This would suggest that children with LD have difficulties with step 1 (encoding social cues) and step 2 (interpretation of cues) of Dodge's model. These findings were again consistent with and supplement the findings of the earlier study examining performance at each of the SIP steps (Nabuzoka, 1993). As we saw, children with LD, compared with non-LD peers, generated fewer possible solutions to a peer group entry situation (step 3), were less accurate in evaluating responses (step 4), and were rated as less competent in enacting peer group entry behaviour (step 5). Tur-Kaspa and Bryan (1994), in another study also examining each step of the SIP model, found that students with LD were less skilled than non-LD (average achieving) classmates at each step. Taken together, these findings indicate difficulties or delays in the social cognitive development of children with LD.

Conclusions

Overall, studies suggest that children with LD have some limitations in their social cognitive functioning that are characterized by developmental delays in aspects of social information processing. Such problems in social cognitive functioning may account for behavioural outcomes that may be associated with the quality of social relations experienced by these children. The theoretical linkages between social information processing steps up to the selection and enactment of a response are largely supported by research findings. These linkages are reflected even when there is some functional differentiation between

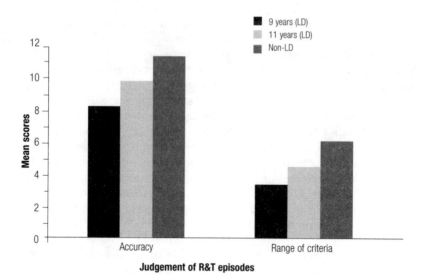

Figure 4.1 *Rough-and-tumble episodes correctly identified and range of criteria used (Nabuzoka and Smith, 1999)*

children. This differentiation is developmental, whether between young and older children with LD, or between chronologically same children with LD and non-LD children.

Thus, developmentally more advanced children identify and use relevant situational cues to a greater extent than do developmentally less advanced children. Similar differences in ability to interpret the presented cues have been indicated. Having identified and interpreted the cues, the same differentiation would apply in the scope of possible solutions generated for the perceived situation. Developmentally more advanced children would generate more solutions and, or if not more, the majority of them would be competent solutions. The developmentally less advanced children, on the other hand, would either generate less solutions and, or if more, fewer of them would be competent ones. Having generated potential solutions, the developmentally more advanced children would make more accurate evaluations of the efficacy and consequences of the potential solutions and make more optimal choices, thus making them likely to enact a more appropriate response than developmentally less advanced children.

Having established that the social cognitive skills of children with LD may be less developed than those of non-LD children, the question of interest is whether such differences do actually account for the quality of social relations experienced by the two groups of children. In particular, the link between social cognition and behaviour *across various situations* needs to be clarified. For example, it has been observed that some non-LD children may function competently in some situations but less competently in others (Dodge and Feldman, 1990). Such variations suggest that the relationship between social cognitive functioning and behaviour of children with LD may not be so straight forward.

Social cognition and behaviour

As indicated earlier, the SIP model of social competence explains behaviour as a product of one's registering and interpretation of social cues, accessing and evaluation of potential responses, and eventual choice of an optimal response. The relationship between such social cognitive and behavioural measures suggests that deficient or inefficient processing of social information may be associated with inappropriate behaviour.

In non-LD children, however, such a relationship may not always hold. Inappropriate behaviour might be attributable to deficient or inefficient processing of social information only in some situations, whilst in other situations it might reflect the cunning manipulation of highly competent individuals. It has been argued, for example, that some children who are bullies may actually belong to the latter category, despite bullying behaviour being generally considered to be inappropriate (Sutton *et al.*, 1999). As children with LD may be less accurate in social information processing, such children's behaviour should differ from that of non-LD children in ways consistent with social cognitive deficiencies. The particular ways in which deficient interpersonal understanding contributes to the social and behavioural problems of children with LD has been a focus of research during the last decade or so (Bender and Smith, 1990; Kavale and Forness, 1996; Kravetz *et al.*, 1999). However, a clearer picture of the nature of this relationship is only just emerging.

Kravetz and colleagues reported a study investigating the extent to which interpersonal understanding mediates the relationship between LD and social behaviour in the classroom. Children with and children without a diagnosis of LD completed a semi-structured developmental clinical interview measure of interpersonal understanding. Teachers also rated the children on typical behaviour deemed to reflect social adaptation in the classroom. The findings of the study indicated a positive correlation between interpersonal understanding and social behaviour in the classroom as a measure of social adaptation. Children with LD were found to exhibit less interpersonal understanding and social adaptation. The group difference on social adaptation was greatly reduced when interpersonal understanding was controlled statistically, but remained statistically significant. This would suggest that interpersonal understanding accounts for a large measure of the behaviour of children with LD. However, this appears to be only partly so. Kravetz and coworkers concluded that reduced social adaptation in the classroom and lower interpersonal understanding may both be associated with a diagnosis of LD. However, they considered the evidence inconclusive for interpersonal understanding mediating the relationship between LD and social behaviour.

Those results suggest that variables other than social cognitive factors are involved. One possible explanation may lie in the differences in the contexts to which the social cognitive and behavioural measures referred. In the study, teachers were asked to rate the frequency of occurrence of 'typical classroom behaviour' on a scale from 1 (never) to 5 (very often). The scale was based on Schaefer and Edgerton's (1978) classroom behaviour inventory and provides scores in ten areas. These include personality, verbal intelligence, creativity, curiosity, consideration, hostility, introversion–extraversion, goal orientation, distractibility, and independence–dependence. In the study, classroom teachers rated the children on only those items related to consideration and hostility as constituting social adaptation. The behaviours tapped by such items are, however, likely to be affected not only by the cognitive functioning of the child, but also by the context.

It has been suggested that while assessment of SIP in one situation may lead to an accurate prediction of social behaviour in that situation, it will predict little about social behaviour in a different type of situation (Dodge and Feldman, 1990). In the Kravetz *et al.* (1999) study, the measures of interpersonal understanding involved a child's appreciation of different aspects of a social problem faced by a hypothetical friend near home (adapted from Selman and Byrne, 1974). However, the behaviours associated with such social cognitive measures were in a different context, that of the classroom. Behaviour of children with LD in the school setting is likely to be affected not only by their social cognitive abilities but also by such factors as their social emotional adjustment as related to academic difficulties.

Social cognition and social adjustment

Numerous researchers have tried to establish the extent to which social information processing, or aspects of it, may be related to such variables as sociometric status (see Chapter 1). These studies, conducted mostly with non-LD children, have generally yielded results supporting a link between social cognition and social outcomes.

A review by Dodge and Feldman (1990) indicated that a number of studies on children's social cognition have yielded significant differences between children with high or low sociometric status. Amongst a number of differences are findings that, compared with more popular children, unpopular children are less skilful at interpreting cues, they generate more deviant responses to interpersonal dilemmas, their skill in evaluating responses is relatively deficient, and their enactment of responses is more incompetent. The findings that children with LD tend to be more unpopular than non-LD children, and that they are less skilful at social information processing, would be consistent with the notion of a link between social cognitive functioning and adjustment. The question of interest is whether sociometric status (popular or unpopular) of children with LD can *necessarily* be accounted for by their social cognitive functioning (such as social information processing). If it can be, to what extent is this relationship significant?

As the relationship between social cognitive functioning and social outcomes (adjustment) is hypothesized to be through the perceived behaviour of children with LD, a theory of such a link must establish a set of other relations. Thus, social cognitive functioning should be related to social behaviour, social behaviour should be related to social outcomes such as sociometric status, and social cognitive functioning should also be related to social outcomes. Regarding the relationship between social cognition and behaviour, we have seen that, while some evidence for such a link does exit (Kravetz *et al.*, 1999), other factors may account for specific behaviours seen in children with LD. The evidence for the relationship between social behaviour and social outcomes is discussed fully in Chapter 5. To be considered in this section is the extent to which the observed relations between social cognitive functioning and social status can be generalized to children with LD as a population.

Dodge and Feldman (1990) pointed out that there are few universal relations between social cognition and status and that most relations tend to be population-specific. They see the task for any theory of social cognition and sociometric status as to explain why one set of relationships holds for one population and another set holds for a second population. Children with LD definitely constitute one population for whom some relationships that hold for non-LD children may not hold. Other factors that are important moderators of the relationship between social cognition and sociometric status are sex and age of the children, as well as the social situations in which these variables are being assessed. A consideration of how these variables may interact with LD status to explain the relationship between social cognition and sociometric status is therefore important. However, before discussing the significance of each of these variables, let us first consider the specific nature of the relationship between social cognition and sociometric status for children with LD.

Linking social cognition and sociometric status

One main conclusion that may be drawn from various studies is that children with LD are relatively more unpopular (with lower social acceptance and sociometric status) than non-LD children, and that this is related to their social cognitive functioning. Though the evidence linking popularity and social cognitive functioning is largely correlational, there is a great temptation to attribute social cognitive deficits to unpopular children. Thus the generally lower sociometric status of children with LD would be attributed to social cognitive deficits. However, children could be unpopular for different reasons, and two of these may be particularly important.

First, children may be unpopular for certain characteristics and/or behaviours not related to social cognitive deficits. One example is of those children who are considered to be bullies. Such children tend to be liked least by their peers and therefore generally unpopular (Nabuzoka and Smith, 1993). However, as argued recently by Sutton *et al.* (1999), bullying behaviour can be perpetrated by children with social cognitive sophistication involving the manipulation of others for their ends. At the other end, physical attractiveness and even being sporty have been associated with popularity. There are also some indications that peer- and teacher-perceived academic competence is associated with social acceptance (Gottlieb *et al.*, 1978).

Second, even where unpopular children have social cognitive deficits, there might be heterogeneity in the nature of such deficits among the children. Individual differences between children who are unpopular may mean that a child may display a deviant or deficient social cognitive pattern in one area, whereas another unpopular child may display a deviant pattern in another area (Dodge and Feldman, 1990). Categorizing children with LD as generally unpopular and with associated social cognitive deficits may also not be wholly accurate. This is because there is some evidence that not all children with LD have problems in social relations, and that social understanding may be more difficult for one category of children with LD but not for another (Rourke, 1989). There are, therefore, individual differences in the extent and specific areas in which social cognitive difficulties may be experienced by children with LD. Where such difficulties exist they may account for a significant amount of social difficulties experienced by such children. However, a recognition of heterogeneity of the type, nature and extent of difficulties that may be faced by children with LD is important for those involved in designing social cognitive interventions as a means of improving their sociometric status.

Sex differences

Sex is one variable that may account for differences on social cognitive measures and sociometric status of children with LD. Sex differences in learning difficulties have been known for some time (Rutter and Yule, 1977), but there is now some evidence that there are similar differences on sociometric status and measures of social cognition.

On some measures, sex seems to interact with LD status such that differences that obtain for non-LD children may not obtain for children with LD or vice versa. For example, boys have been found to be more likely than girls to be rejected on measures of sociometric status for non-LD children (Coie *et al.*, 1982). Amongst children with LD, however, rejection has been found to be particularly stronger for girls than for boys (Kistner and Gatlin, 1989a). Studies of social cognition in boys and girls have demonstrated some sex differences among non-LD children (Shantz, 1983). Girls seem to be superior to boys in social perspective-taking and affective empathy (Zahn-Waxler *et al.*, 1977). Hoffman (1977) suggested that girls, more than boys, were socialized both to be attentive to the needs of others and to put themselves in another person's position. This observation was supported by findings in a study by Kurdek and Krile (1982), in which girls were found to perform better than boys on Selman's (1980) measures of interpersonal understanding.

Age trends

Age is another important variable to be considered. One hypothesis is that low-status children are lagging in the development of social cognitive skills relative to their peers (Garber, 1984). If children with LD generally have low sociometric status, one could reasonably speculate, on the basis of this hypothesis, that such children should lag behind their non-LD peers on social cognitive skills. This can be tested by matching non-LD children and children with LD on age and then measuring the social cognitive skills and sociometric status for each group.

Support for such a social cognitive developmental lag for children with LD may be suggested by poorer performance on the social cognitive measures and lower sociometric status. But support for the developmental lag hypothesis would need also to show age trends among children with LD, and not just differences relative to similarly aged non-LD children.

Among non-LD children, the hypothesis that low-status children perform similarly to younger children has been supported in some social cognitive domains. These include encoding search (Dodge and Newman, 1982) and intention cue detection accuracy (Dodge *et al.*, 1984). The latter study examined the ability to discriminate among types of peer intentions by children in kindergarten (pre-school), second-grade (7-year-olds), and fourth grade (9-year-olds). These children were identified by sociometric measures as having peer status as 'popular', 'average', 'socially rejected' or 'socially neglected'. The measure involved videos in which one child provoked another child, but with the intention of the first child being varied across episodes. Intentions of the first child depicted on the videos included being hostile, prosocial, accidental, ambiguous, or merely present. Dodge and colleagues found scores on this measure to increase as a function of increasing age. In addition, they found that popular and average children scored more highly than children who were neglected or rejected. The children who were neglected or rejected tended to label prosocial intentions erroneously as hostile. Furthermore, children's statements about what would be their responses to provocations by peers were found to vary as a function of their perceptions of the intentions of the peer, and not as a function of the actual intention portrayed. These responses could also be distinguished by sociometric status differences of the children.

The findings by Dodge and coworkers are consistent with the hypothesis of a developmental lag among low-status children in the acquisition of intention cue detection skills. Similar evidence for a developmental lag among children with LD has been found on studies of social perception (Gerber and Zinkgraf, 1982; Nabuzoka and Smith, 1995) and social information processing (Nabuzoka, 1993). Studies that have directly examined the relationship between sociometric measures and social cognitive measures among children with LD are not easily identifiable. However, on the basis of evidence for lower sociometric status for children with LD relative to non-LD peers, and developmental delays on measures of social cognitive functioning, it is reasonable to speculate that a developmental lag in social cognitive skills accounts for a significant variance in the low status of children with LD.

The role of the social situation

It was indicated earlier that assessment of social cognitive functioning in one situation might predict behaviour in that situation, but not necessarily also in a different situation. This suggests not only that the relationship between social cognitive functioning and behaviour is situation-specific, but also that the social situation affects social cognitive functioning.

Two aspects of the social situation may be relevant here. One relates to the contextual features of the setting in which functioning is being assessed. The other relates to the content of the social situations themselves. Contextual features may relate to the classroom, the playground or the laboratory, while the content of the situation may relate to such aspects as conflict versus non-conflict situations, peer group entry, or initiation of friendships. The content of the situation relates more directly to the child's task at hand, while the context sets the scene for the task. Both the content and contextual features of the situation can have a strong effect on the social cognitive performance of a child.

Children with LD may be particularly susceptible to variations in social cognitive functioning across situations. It has been suggested, for example, that deficits in decoding social situations may lead to children with LD not being able to understand when to perform certain behaviours (Perlmutter, 1986). However, such deficits may not be as easily identifiable in the classroom as in the playground.

Nabuzoka and Smith (1993) pointed out that the classroom situation is relatively easier to decode than the playground, as the social roles are more clearly defined in the former. What is expected of every child in the classroom is made explicitly clear, mostly by teachers who are (one hopes) in control. On the other hand, the situations during free-play in the playground or in the corridors are relatively unstructured. A multitude of social cognitive skills are required in such situations. For example, a child may require knowledge of social rules for turn-taking and reciprocity (necessary in maintaining social interaction and in rough-and-tumble play), and handling interpersonal conflict (such as when faced with bullying). The range of skills required in these situations may be too demanding cognitively, and so may not be as easy for children with LD to decode.

Problems in decoding social situations can often lead to inappropriate responses that contribute to unpopularity. Unpopularity as a sociometric measure is an enduring attribute that may be identifiable across a variety of assessment situations and may even be self-perpetuating (Cillessen, 1991). However, the social cognitive correlates of such status may not be easily identifiable if a child's level of functioning in this domain varies as a function of the situation. In this respect, assessment of social cognitive functioning may not always accurately predict sociometric status as a measure of social adjustment. Conversely, measures of social cognitive functioning limited to specific social situations such as the classroom may be poor predictors of the overall social adjustment of a child.

Summary and conclusions

This chapter has examined some social cognitive processes and overall social understanding of children with LD. The social information processing model proposed by Dodge and his colleagues has been useful in evaluating this aspect of social competence. There are some indications that the social problems of children with LD may not be due just to an inability to perceive social information, but also to impairment at any of the stages of interpretation, accessing of an appropriate response, or even the enactment of an appropriate response. Research examining the process by which each individual child arrives at a given behavioural enactment from perception of social cues supports this view.

This research indicates some limitations in the social cognitive functioning of children with LD when compared with non-LD peers. However, social cognitive factors may not be sufficient to explain the social adjustment of children with LD as a specific population. There are some indications that, along with social cognitive factors, the behavioural attributes associated with social adjustment may be accounted for by factors such as those related to the social–emotional well-being of the child. In addition, other factors may moderate a link between social cognition and outcomes such as sociometric status for children with LD. These other factors include sex, age and the social situation.

In some cases, social adjustment outcomes such as sociometric status may be related to social cognitive abilities in much more complex ways than suggested by a social cognitive deficit hypothesis. Such complexity may be unravelled by examining the type of behavioural attributes of children with LD that are associated with social adjustment, and determining the underlining social cognitive implications of such behaviours.

Chapter 5

Behavioural characteristics associated with social adjustment

As we saw in the last two chapters, social perceptual and cognitive abilities may be associated with social adjustment. It has also been suggested that these are related to behavioural attributes of children with learning disabilities (LD), which would account for the quality of social relations experienced by these children. One task for researchers, therefore, has been to establish the extent to which behavioural attributes of children with LD may be associated with the quality of their social relations or social adjustment. Sociometric status is one measure of social adjustment often used.

The sociometric status of a child defines his or her social experiences in the peer group. Theoretically, a child who is neglected or rejected may generally be isolated and thereby have negative experiences such as loneliness or anxiety. This in turn can have a bearing on a child's behaviour patterns in ways that may reinforce his or her low sociometric status.

The implication, of course, is that it becomes difficult to determine whether some behavioural attributes serve as a cause or consequence of social adjustment. Either can be the case for an individual child with LD, and determining which is the case is important as it has implications for intervention. If negative sociometric status arises from behavioural attributes, intervention aimed at changing behaviour might improve the sociometric status. Conversely, improving the sociometric status of a child may promote positive behaviour. The main task for researchers of social development and preventive intervention, however, is to determine the particular nature and manifestation of this relationship between behaviour and sociometric status.

Studies on non-LD children have established and elaborated on the relationship between children's behavioural attributes and their sociometric status (Coie *et al.*, 1990; Hartup, 1983; Hymel and Rubin, 1985). This chapter examines some behavioural aspects of social functioning specifically related to LD status and their relationship to social adjustment as reflected in sociometric status and acceptance. Research that identifies behavioural characteristics that distinguish children with LD from non-LD peers, and are associated with such aspects of social adjustment, is reviewed and discussed. The implications of specific behavioural attributes for the social cognitive development of children with LD, and the theoretical and practical implications of the findings, are also discussed.

Linking behaviour and social adjustment

Several studies have focused on behavioural correlates of peer relations to explain the problems faced by children with LD (e.g. Bryan and Bryan, 1981; Nabuzoka and Smith, 1993). These studies have been influenced by similar work linking behaviour and peer rejection in typically developing, non-LD children (Coie *et al.*, 1990). It has been suggested that behavioural differences between children with LD and non-LD children become visible through comparison with peers in integrated settings. Such differences are thought to contribute to the social isolation of children with disabilities (Gottlieb, 1981). For example, children with LD have been associated with higher levels of aggressive and disruptive behaviour (Foster *et al.*, 1985). These negative or inappropriate behaviours are thought to be a central feature of problems faced by such children (McConaughy and Ritter, 1986) and to account for their social isolation, rejection or negative status.

Views have been influenced by a number of assumptions regarding the social functioning of children with LD. First, it has been held that there is a relationship between learning (or intellectual) disability and behavioural problems: children with LD as a group have been seen as characterized by aggressive, disruptive or negative behaviour in comparison with typically developing children (Jorm *et al.*, 1986; McMichael, 1980; Sturge, 1982). Second, there is a body of evidence linking negative behaviours with negative sociometric status amongst non-LD populations (Dodge *et al.*, 1982; Dodge, 1983; French, 1988). A similar association has thus been made between negative behaviours and low social status of many children with LD.

However, not all children with LD experience social problems or have negative social status. Indeed, children with LD are not a homogeneous group characterized by certain types of behaviour. There appears to be a subgroup of children with learning or intellectual disability who show negative or antisocial behavioural characteristics, and this group may be at risk for difficulties in peer relations. Thus, those children with LD who are perceived by peers and teachers as misbehaving tend to be more rejected by their non-LD peers than do those who are not misbehaving (Gottlieb, *et al.*, 1978). Flicek and Landau (1985), for example, classified third- through sixth-grade students (8- to 11-year-olds) as hyperactive and non-hyperactive, and compared the social status of the two subgroups with that of a control group of non-LD children. The findings indicated that the hyperactive children with LD were significantly less popular and significantly more rejected than either the non-hyperactive children with LD or the non-LD children. In addition, peers and teachers rated the hyperactive subgroup of children with LD as engaging in more negative and aggressive behaviour than non-LD or non-hyperactive children with LD.

Studies reported by McMichael (1980) and Taylor (1990) indicated similar findings. McMichael compared good and poor readers differing in their social behaviour and found that poor readers who exhibited antisocial behaviour patterns were significantly more rejected than poor readers and good readers who showed stable social behaviour patterns. In the study by Taylor (1990), low-achieving second- through fifth-grade students (7- to 10-year-olds) were identified and matched with a sample of average achieving children. Peer assessment measures of co-operative, disruptive, aggressive, and shy behaviour were used to identify behavioural subtypes of low-achieving children. Results showed two distinct subtypes of low-achieving children: an aggressive–disruptive group and a non-aggressive but somewhat shy group. The low-achieving, aggressive–disruptive children were found to be less socially accepted and more rejected than the average-achieving children. They were also rated by teachers as having more difficulty handling problematic social situations than either average-achieving children or low-achieving, non-aggressive children. The low-achieving, non-aggressive children did not differ from average-achieving children in peer sociometric status or in their ability to handle social problem situations.

The data from these studies therefore suggest a link between negative behaviours and lack of social acceptance only for some, but not necessarily all, children with LD. For this subgroup of children with LD, poor peer relations may be associated with such negative behaviours. This is not to say, however, that the children's problems in social relations are caused by their behaviour as either could be a cause or consequence of the other. It is also possible that both a lack of social acceptance and negative behaviours could be consequences of some other factors. Furthermore, there has been some indication that some children with LD, but without antisocial behaviour problems, may still experience poorer peer relations than their non-LD counterparts. For example, the study by McMichael (1980) found that non-antisocial poor readers were still significantly less accepted than stable good readers.

Flicek and Landau (1985) also found that non-hyperactive children with LD were significantly less popular and more rejected than the non-LD children. Taylor (1990), on the other hand, did not find any sociometric status differences between non-aggressive, low-achieving children and average-achieving children. It would seem, therefore, that while antisocial behaviour may be a strong predictor of peer rejection, other characteristics may account for low social status of the subgroup of children with LD who are not particularly antisocial. Such characteristics may or may not be in the behavioural domain. One explanation is that it is the combination of learning or intellectual disability with behavioural problems that significantly contributes to peer rejection of children with LD.

Given that not all children with LD necessarily fall into the same status categories (Ochoa and Palmer, 1991), and that some behavioural characteristics may vary within this group of children, some researchers have sought to identify and further clarify which behavioural profiles are related to the different social status of children with LD. However, few studies have directly sought to identify behavioural characteristics specific to children with LD that might explain their social problems. One central question, for example, is whether rejected or isolated children with LD have behavioural profiles similar to those of non-LD children similarly categorized. Identification of which behaviours are associated with which status, and whether these differ for children with LD and non-LD children with similar status, is important as it will enable more accurate targeting of intervention programmes. On the other hand, if similar behavioural profiles are associated with similar status for the two groups of children, similar intervention approaches could be considered. Some studies have therefore focused on identification of the status groups into which children with LD fall, the behavioural profiles associated with such status, and whether these differ from those of typically developing (non-LD) children.

Research evidence linking social behaviour and sociometric status of children with LD has typically involved children with LD being compared with non-LD children on peer nominations to various behavioural categories, and on the dimensions of social preference and social impact. Behavioural measures of peer preferences and quality of interactions have also been obtained through direct observation of social behaviour. In some studies, peer behavioural nominations and/or teacher evaluations of social behaviour have been used. In other cases, these have been compared or supplemented with direct observations of social interaction patterns. In the next sections, some of these types of study are examined separately and their findings discussed.

Behaviour observed in school settings

Observational studies in school settings have focused on two types of interaction: between children and adults (mostly teachers or careworkers), and between specific children with other children. This section looks briefly at interactions involving teachers, and then examines more closely the interactions between children. The context for the former is often, though not exclusively, in the classroom, while the latter may occur outside that formal setting. As we shall see later, this can have implications for the nature of behaviour that may occur, or indeed be recognized as characteristic of individual children.

As we saw in Chapter 2, a number of studies indicate that children with LD may experience a different type of interaction with teachers from that experienced by non-LD peers (Pearl *et al.*, 1986). In some studies, for example, children with LD have been observed to interact more with teachers than do non-LD children (Roberts *et al.*, 1991; Siperstein and Goding, 1983). In such cases teachers tend to be more directive and corrective towards the children with LD than they are with non-LD children (Siperstein and Goding, 1983). It is likely that such patterns of interactions may reflect difficulties in attending to tasks by children with LD. For example, these children have been found to be more off-task or distractible (Feagans and McKinney, 1981; Roberts *et al.*, 1991). However, the significance of such attention accorded to children with LD is that it could be a source of resentment by non-LD children and thus may contribute to negative perceptions of the children with LD (Lynas, 1986).

Turning now to peer interactions, a number of studies have found no differences between children with LD and non-LD children in the amount of time spent in interaction with classmates (Pearl *et al.*, 1986; Roberts *et al.*, 1991). This suggests that the quantity of peer interactions does not distinguish the children with LD from their classmates. But do these groups of children differ in the types of social behaviour displayed? Roberts *et al.* (1991) compared children with LD and non-LD children on observed classroom and playground behaviour. They found that the frequencies of negative behaviour during interaction in the classroom and playground settings were low and did not differ across the two groups of children. The children with disabilities did not engage in any more disruptive or negative behaviour than did their peers. In addition, no significant difference was found between the groups of children in their peer initiation patterns. This latter finding would suggest that children with LD can be as proactive as non-LD children in social interaction. An earlier study reported by Bryan (1974a) had similarly indicated that children with LD do initiate interactions with classmates. However, the children with LD were more likely than non-LD peers in similar positions to be ignored. It would seem that children with LD make efforts to interact with their non-LD peers but, for some reason, such efforts are either not attended to or are rebuffed.

Why should this be? It is clear that it cannot be explained solely by the type of behaviour shown by children with LD. As we saw, some studies have not found significant differences between children with

LD and non-LD children on some negative behaviours. On the other hand, differences between the two groups of children in patterns of positive social behaviours are not very clear. Some studies have not found any differences (Bryan *et al.*, 1976), while others have suggested that children with LD display more positive social behaviour than do non-LD peers (Bryan, 1978). If positive behaviours are associated with positive regard, children displaying positive behaviours should be regarded positively by peers. This, however, seems not to be the case for some children with LD. In one study for example, Sainato *et al.* (1983) reported that the frequency with which children with LD made positive initiations was negatively related to their sociometric status. This would suggest that it is not just the frequency of positive or negative behaviour that may be associated with the social adjustment of children with LD.

Another possible explanation is that there are qualitative differences in behaviours by the two groups of children. Roberts *et al.* (1991) suggested that even though children with disabilities did not engage in any more disruptive or negative behaviour than their peers, they may still be viewed by their peers as cognitively less competent and therefore less desirable as mates. Some studies suggest that this may be due to subtle differences in behaviour, especially regarding the *quality* of communications with peers (Pearl *et al.*, 1986). Communication problems of children with LD, for example, can involve both verbal and non-verbal cues (Spafford and Grosser, 1993): the former as transmitted by children with LD and the latter as read by them. As we saw in Chapter 3, individuals with LD are relatively poorer than non-LD peers in understanding non-verbal social cues such as body language or gestures (Nabuzoka and Smith, 1995; Sisterhen and Gerber, 1989). Such failure to detect social interaction cues or prompts could result in behaviour that is inappropriate even though not particularly disruptive. For example, children with LD have been found to be less responsive in interpersonal interactions (Mathinos, 1991).

Studies assessing the conversational behaviour of children with LD also indicate that, even though they actively try to communicate with peers, others may not easily understand them (Donahue and Bryan, 1983). Although the oral expressive language of individuals with LD may be similar in mechanics and range of utterances, they introduce some speech production errors that make their interpersonal interactions less consistent, appropriate and flexible (Speckman, 1981). Children with LD have also been found to be less skilful in sustaining a conversation (Bryan *et al.*, 1981b) and to converse in a deferential, unassertive manner (Bryan *et al.*, 1981a) while at times they may give the impression of being more hostile. The quality of the conversational behaviour of children with LD, in terms of appropriateness of the responses or utterances to the context, may thus give peers an impression of being cognitively less competent.

Studies on the conversational behaviour of children with LD suggest, in this respect, that these children do in fact engage in behaviour that may lead others to react negatively. They apparently emit more negative statements to peers (for example, more competitive, more very nasty, more rejecting comments). These children, as a result of such predisposition, are recipients of more negative comments and fewer consideration statements from peers (Bryan *et al.*, 1976). It is these observations that have led such children to be categorized as generally engaging in more negative and rejecting interactions with peers (LaGreca, 1981). The negative connotations in such interactions appear to be mostly in the tone and general orientations of verbalizations.

Some of these negative verbal interaction categories have been shown to be related to low peer status. In particular, research reviewed by LaGreca (1981) showed that children who were rejected by peers (those who scored highly on measures of peer rejection, and low on peer acceptance) directed more negative statements to peers than did children who had more positive peer status (i.e. who were less rejected and/or more accepted). The findings also seemed to suggest that differential social behaviours are related to a child's peer acceptance status, and not to LD status *per se*. The relationship between social behaviour and sociometric status or acceptance of children with LD, as particularly differentiated from that relating to non-LD children, is examined more closely later in this chapter.

Differences in verbal styles have also been attributed to the type of situation. In highly structured situations where the expected verbalizations are fairly evident, children with LD tend to comply with the expected behaviour, but in a deferential and unassertive manner. In situations with ambiguous expectations, the communications of children with LD has at times appeared more negative (Pearl *et al.*, 1986). One explanation is that ambiguous situations may be more cognitively demanding for children with LD and as such more difficult for the children to decode and decide on appropriate responses. It has been suggested, for example, that children with LD are generally capable of performing appropriate behaviours but only lack the ability to understand when it is appropriate for them to be performed. This would be consistent with the notion of social cognitive factors being implicated in the behavioural orientations of children with LD (see Chapters 3 and 4).

Conclusion
Children with LD may not always be withdrawn or isolated in their interactions with others. They have been observed to initiate and even participate in interactions with other children as much as non-LD children. However, these children may not be appropriately responsive to other people's overtures, and the tone of their behaviour apparently often differs from that typical of others such that they may be ignored

or rebuffed. This may be a result of social misperception and impaired communication skills of children with LD (Spafford and Grosser, 1993). Thus, differences in the quality of social behaviour may be responsible for difficulties experienced in social relations as evidenced by the low regard with which children with LD are held (Gresham and Reschly, 1986).

Making such a link between behaviour and *quality* of social relations of children with LD implies that such children are *perceived* to behave differently by their non-LD peers, and that such perceptions account for acceptance or rejection The next section examines whether this is the case, and the extent to which direct links can be established between such perceived behaviour and social status.

Peer assessments of behaviour and sociometric status

Observing the patterns of social interaction between children with LD and their peers can provide information about the behavioural skills of the children, and whether children with LD participate fully in peer group activities. Inferences can then be made about the relationship between behaviours and patterns of interactions observed. For example, if children with LD are observed to be less responsive to overtures of non-LD peers and tend to be generally solitary or isolated, we could infer that a relationship exists between the children's behavioural orientation (responsiveness) and sociometric status ('neglected'). However, such studies can enable us only to make inferences regarding the relationship between the sociometric status of the children observed and their behavioural skills. What may not be clear, but important for researchers concerned with preventive intervention, is which of the observed behaviours are considered by peers as significantly characteristic of individual children and thus influence their responses to them. Such measures can be obtained directly from the children by asking them to indicate both their peer preferences – such as who they like most or least – and corresponding behavioural characteristics associated with each of their peers.

This section reviews some studies that have examined peer assessments of behaviour and corresponding sociometric status. First, study measures typically used are outlined and discussed, including the procedures for collecting data and behavioural categories. Some studies focusing on behavioural differences between children with LD and non-LD peers are then reviewed. Data is discussed showing the relationship between behaviour and sociometric status for children with and without LD, and separately for each group. Finally, an attempt is made to identify some of the behavioural characteristics that peers associate with children with LD.

Measures

Studies of peer assessments of behaviour typically use nomination methods (Coie *et al.*, 1982; Parker and Asher, 1987; Parkhurst and Asher, 1992). Peers are asked to nominate a child or a number of children from their class who best fit a specified set of behavioural characteristics. In studies of sociometric status or acceptance, the peer nomination and peer rating methods (Asher and Dodge, 1986) have been used to quantify the degree to which a child is liked or not liked by peers. The peer rating method typically yields a measure of the social acceptance of children. It involves obtaining children's scores regarding the degree to which they may hold positive attitudes towards peers. The peer nomination method, on the other hand, yields a measure of the qualitatively different sociometric positions that exist in a group of children. As the peer nomination method can be used for both assessments of peer perceptions of behaviour and sociometric status, it has been found to be useful for comparing the relationship between perceived behavioural attributes and sociometric status.

These studies typically involve the participating children being interviewed individually. In the interview, it is first established that the child knows all the other children. In a number of cases the child is shown a list of classmates' names and asked to go through it together with the experimenter. In some cases photographs of classmates may be used. These are used to establish that the child knows all the children who can be nominated. For sociometric measures, and after establishing that the child knows every other child, he or she is then asked to indicate a number of children they like most, and children they like least. Some studies have focused on same-gender classmates while in other studies children may be told they can pick a child of any gender. Depending on the proportions of 'like most' and 'like least' nominations received by a child, they are classified into one of the following categories: 'popular', 'rejected', 'neglected', 'controversial', or 'average'.

In most studies, the procedure for classifying children into sociometric categories has closely followed that of Coie *et al.* (1982). Thus, the frequencies of positive nominations ('like most') and negative nominations ('like least') for each child are computed and transformed into standardized liking (L) and disliking (D) scores within each classroom. A social preference (SP) score is then computed as the standard L score minus the standard D score, and a social impact (SI) score is computed as the sum of the standard L and D scores. The SP and SI scores are then standardized within each classroom. Each child is then classified as fitting one of the following groups:

- *popular*, receiving an SP score greater than 1.0, an L score greater than 0, and a D score less than 0;

- *rejected*, receiving an *SP* score less than –1.0, an *L* score less than 0, and a *D* score greater than 0;
- *neglected*, receiving an *SI* score less than –1.0, an *L* score less than 0, and a *D* score less than 0;
- *controversial*, receiving an *SI* score greater than 1.0, an *L* score greater than 0, and a *D* score greater than 0;
- *average*, receiving an *SP* score between –0.5 and 0.5 and an *SI* score between –0.5 and 0.5;
- *other* – all the remaining children.

In order to determine the relationship between sociometric status and behaviour, each child is asked to nominate a number of children who best fit each description of some behavioural category. This may be conducted at the same time as the sociometric nominations are being obtained.

In studies of typically developing (non-LD) children, some behavioural correlates of status have been found to be consistent across different age levels (Coie *et al.*, 1990). For example, Coie and colleagues reported that being co-operative, and other prosocial behaviours, often emerge as major correlates of positive status at each age studied. Aggression, on the other hand, is the primary correlate of negative status at all ages. The nature of such behaviour, however, changes with age. The processes involved in behaving co-operatively and prosocially appear to become increasingly complex as children become older. The nature of aggressiveness also changes with age: while hitting and name-calling constitute aggressiveness at younger ages, aggressiveness at older ages becomes more differentiated and less overt. The developmental significance of such patterns of behaviour has implications for the social adjustment of children with LD whose level of functioning may differ from that of peers.

Bullying is another type of behaviour associated with sociometric status. In recent times, great importance has been attached to problems of bullying, especially with regard to their implications for social adjustment (Olweus, 1991; Smith, 1991). As indicated in Chapter 2, children who are alone at playtime, or do not have many friends, run the risk of being victims. If children with LD tend to be in the 'neglected' or 'rejected' categories of sociometric status, as shown in a number of studies, they are also likely to be over-represented as victims of bullying. On the other hand, those children with LD who have behavioural problems may act in an aggressive way and be perceived by peers as either bullies or 'provocative victims' (i.e. meeting criteria for being regarded as both bullies and victims of bullying). Given the link between aggression and peer rejection, such children would be expected to fall in the 'rejected' category.

Thus, behavioural categories found to be particularly useful in examining the relationship between behaviour and sociometric status in non-LD children include descriptions of a child who, in the context of the peer group, 'co-operates', is 'disruptive', 'fights', 'bullies others', or is a 'bullying victim'. These behaviours have similarly been used to study peer perceptions of children with LD. In addition to these, other behaviours have particular significance for children with LD as reflected in observed patterns of interaction characteristic of such children. These include descriptions of a child who 'is shy', 'seeks help' or often takes the initiative in the peer group and is thus 'a leader'.

Behavioural differences between children with LD and their peers

One attempt at identifying differences in behavioural characteristics between children with LD and non-LD peers, and to account for differences in sociometric status between the two groups of children, was undertaken by Nabuzoka and Smith (1993). They used peer nominations (after Coie *et al.*, 1982) to various behavioural characteristics. The children were aged 8–12 years and came from two mainstream schools with integrated resources for children with LD. The children with LD attended the same classes as non-LD children. Each child participating in the study was asked to nominate classmates who best fitted each of eight behavioural descriptions of 'co-operates', 'disrupts', 'shy', 'fights', seeks help', 'leader', 'bully' and 'victim'. The total number of nominations received by each child was then determined and standardized within each class.

Nabuzoka and Smith found that children with LD were nominated as shy, seeking help and as victims of bullying to a significantly larger extent than non-LD children. In addition, they received fewer nominations of being co-operative and as a leader. There were no significant differences on nominations of disruptive, fighting and bullying behaviour. These findings are illustrated in Figure 5.1.

Correlations of bully and victim nominations with other behavioural nominations revealed a similar picture for children with and without LD. Bullies were seen as being disruptive and starting fights, and victims were seen as being shy and needing help. These findings suggest that children perceived by peers to be shy and needing help are also more likely to be seen as victims of bullying. Such behavioural characteristics were associated with children with LD significantly more than non-LD children. Children perceived to be disruptive and starting fights were also likely to be seen as bullies, but such behavioural characteristics did not distinguish children with LD from their peers. Thus, children with LD may not be perceived by peers as characterized by more negative and aggressive behaviour than non-LD children, consistent with observational studies. However, children with LD may be perceived by peers to be characterized by vulnerability or inadequacy as reflected in being shy, seeking help and being victims of bullying.

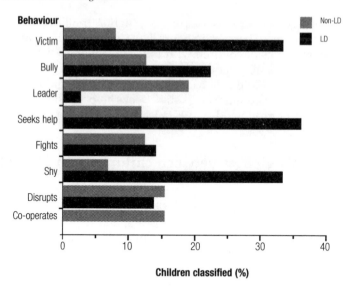

Figure 5.1 *Peer behavioural nominations of children with LD and non-LD children (Nabuzoka and Smith, 1993)*

Relationship between behaviour and sociometric status

Nabuzoka and Smith (1993) also asked the children in their study to nominate classmates they 'like most' and those they 'like least'. The 'like most' and 'like least' nominations yielded classifications of the children into sociometric categories across which the behavioural nominations were compared. The distribution of children with LD across some status groups was found to be significantly different from that of non-LD children. More children with LD than non-LD children were rejected and none were popular. On the other hand, fewer children with LD than non-LD children were neglected (see Figure 5.2). No statistically significant differences were observed in the 'controversial' or 'average' categories.

The finding that children with LD are less popular and more rejected than those without learning difficulties has been consistent across a number of studies (Bryan, 1974b, 1976; Bruininks, 1978; Garrett and Crump, 1980; Horowitz, 1981). However, while a number of studies found children with LD to be more ignored (i.e. neglected), Nabuzoka and Smith (1993) found the opposite on this category: non-LD children tended to be nominated as neglected to a larger extent than children with LD. This finding seems contrary to the general trend in the literature on similar investigations where children with LD have been found to be more neglected.

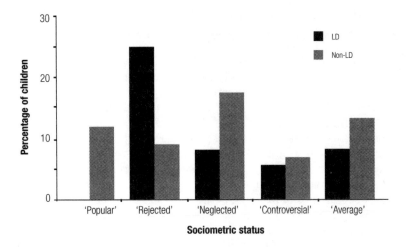

Figure 5.2 *Sociometric status of children with and without LD (Nabuzoka and Smith, 1993)*

Nabuzoka and Smith's findings on the neglected status category, however, become interesting when looked at in relation to the 'rejected' status category. The variation as to whether a child is assigned to one or the other category could be attributed to the method of defining sociometric status. There have been some studies reporting a blurred distinction between these two status categories (Musun-Miller, 1990). Indeed, children who are rejected or neglected are those with few or no nominations of 'liked most'. Both can be said to have few or no close friends. However, children in the 'rejected' category have more 'like least' nominations and fewer 'like most' nominations. Neglected children, on the other hand, would have few 'like most' and few 'like least' nominations. Thus rejected children can be said to be actively disliked while neglected children are largely ignored.

The Coie *et al.* (1982) method of sociometric classification has been shown to be more parsimonious than other methods in assigning children to the 'neglected' category (Terry and Coie, 1991). In this respect, Nabuzoka and Smith's (1993) study seems to indicate that children with LD and non-LD children who are not popular can be clearly distinguished in terms of the 'rejected' and 'neglected' categories. Thus children with few or no close friends (scoring few or no 'liked most' nominations) tend to be rejected if they have LD, and neglected if they are non-LD children. Such differences in the attitudes towards unpopular children in the two diagnostic groups can perhaps be better understood in relation to the perceived behavioural dispositions ascribed to them.

Comparisons of peer nominations to behaviour categories across the social status groups indicated patterns generally consistent with studies on non-LD children (Coie *et al.*, 1982; Coie and Dodge, 1988). 'Popular' children scored higher on being a leader than 'rejected', 'neglected' and 'other' children. They also scored higher on being co-operative than children in the other status groups. 'Controversial' children scored higher on being co-operative than 'rejected' and 'neglected' children. 'Rejected' children scored higher on being disruptive than 'popular', 'neglected' and 'average' children; and higher on starting fights than 'popular', 'neglected' and 'other' children. They also scored higher on bully, victim and seeking-help nominations than each of the other status groups.

In the specific case of bullying behaviour, some studies have shown a relationship between bullying and peer status in typically developing children. For example, Boulton and Smith (1994) examined the sociometric status and perceptions of behavioural descriptions by peers of bullies, victims and not-involved children. The results showed that sociometrically rejected children received both more bully and more victim nominations than other sociometric status groups, while the popular children received less of these kinds of nomination. They also found that bullies, victims and not-involved children were perceived differently on the behavioural descriptions of 'starts fights', 'seeks help', 'leader', 'co-operates', and 'disrupts'. The above evidence suggests that there is a relationship between the bully–victim dimension of children's behaviour and negative sociometric status.

Nabuzoka and Smith (1993) also examined the relationship between such behaviours and 'liked most' and 'liked least' nominations for children with LD and non-LD children separately. The findings were generally in the expected direction, with nominations for being co-operative significantly related to being liked most for both groups of children. However, a significant positive relationship between being liked most and nomination as leader for non-LD children was not significant for children with LD. Nominations for being disruptive, fighting and bullying were significantly related to being liked least for both groups of children. However, seeking help and being a victim of bullying were significantly related to being liked least for non-LD children but not significantly related for children with LD. The differences in correlation of these attributes for children with LD and non-LD children were significant. Thus, behaviours that tended to go with being liked least for children with LD were different from behaviours linked to being liked least for non-LD children. These findings suggest that the behavioural patterns associated with the same sociometric status may be different for children with LD. The latter may thus be judged on different criteria.

Despite some views that children with disabilities may have social problems as a result of their high level of aggressive and disruptive behaviour (Foster *et al.*, 1985), children with LD seem to be perceived not to differ significantly from their peers on behavioural nominations of 'disrupts', 'fights' or 'bully' (Nabuzoka and Smith, 1993). These behaviours are associated with being liked least by peers, and are therefore indicators of negative status for children with and without LD. However, since children with LD tend to be more rejected and not popular, it would seem that peer rejection and lack of popularity of children with LD may not be associated only with aggressive and disruptive behaviour as such. This is consistent with the findings by McMichael (1980) and those by Flicek and Landau (1985) that even non-antisocial and non-hyperactive LD children, respectively, were significantly less accepted than non-LD children. Similar observations made amongst non-LD adolescents (Parkhurst and Asher, 1992) may be relevant here. The latter study found that most rejected students were aggressive or submissive, but it was the combination of aggressiveness and submissiveness with low levels of prosocial behaviour that was associated with peer rejection for non-LD children.

What, then, are the behavioural characteristics that peers associate with children with LD and that make the latter to be more rejected? A number of behavioural differences have been identified. In the study by Nabuzoka and Smith (1993), children with LD were to a larger extent nominated on dimensions which reflected vulnerability or inadequacy (i.e. 'shy', 'seeking help,' and 'victim of bullying') while non-LD children tended to be picked as peers who 'co-operate' and as 'leader.' Being perceived as shy and being perceived as a leader were negatively and positively related, respectively, to being liked most for the non-LD children, but were not significantly related to being liked least for either group of children. The contribution of these behaviours to negative status (rejection and lack of popularity) is therefore questionable. Taylor (1990) found, for example, that being somewhat more shy and withdrawn did not distinguish low-achieving, non-aggressive children from their average-achieving counterparts in social status. Indeed, people are not normally disliked for being shy or lacking leadership qualities. On the other hand, those who have leadership qualities and/or are not shy tend to be largely liked.

The behaviours that seem to distinguish the two groups on this dimension (rejection versus popularity) are those relating to being co-operative, seeking help, and being victims of bullying. These behaviours were found to be significantly related to unpopularity for non-LD children (negatively for being co-operative) but not for children with LD. It is likely that the difference in association could be a result of differences in the range of variation on these behaviours between the two groups. The interesting finding is that seeking help and being victims of bullying are behavioural characteristics in which LD children also tended to be proportionally over-represented. Since these behaviours were associated with being liked least, they probably help explain the peer rejection of children with LD. Being seen as co-operative, on the other hand, was significantly associated with being liked most for children with and without LD. Nabuzoka and Smith (1993) found that none of the children with LD met the criteria for classification as co-operative, and subsequently none of them was in the 'popular' category.

The negative status of children with LD would therefore seem to be related to a perceived general lack of social competence in social interactions as indicated by being seen to be less co-operative, being seen as victims of bullying and being seen as constantly in need of help. The behaviours associated with each of the three behavioural concepts – co-operates, seeks help, and a victim – relate, in their own ways, to competence in handling interpersonal situations. Being co-operative implies competence in interaction as it involves knowledge of social rules for turn-taking and reciprocity (see Strain and Shores, 1977); being a victim of bullying implies vulnerability and a lack of competence in handling interpersonal conflict; and constantly seeking help implies a general lack of self-help as well as social skills. A child who is seen as co-operative is an asset to the peer group; a victim of bullying who cannot stand up for himself/herself, or who constantly requires help in most activities, can be perceived as a burden on the group. In addition, the constant support of teachers required by children with LD in integrated settings can be a source of resentment by their non-LD peers (Lynas, 1986) and hence reinforce the negative view of constantly seeking help.

It is important to bear in mind that the children with LD in these studies have been placed in integrated settings and may therefore mostly include those with minor behavioural problems; the children with more severe problems tend to be placed in special schools. Particularly aggressive children with LD may thus be under-represented in the samples. Nevertheless, such findings do indicate that even where children with LD may not be perceived to differ significantly on aggressive and disruptive behaviour from non-LD peers, they still tend to be over-represented in the category of rejected children. These differences seem to be associated with corresponding differences in behavioural skills that reflect interpersonal competence in peer relations.

Sex differences

Research has generally found consistent sex differences on behavioural nominations (e.g. Coie *et al.*, 1982; Coie and Dodge, 1988, Nabuzoka and Smith, 1993). Boys tend to be nominated to fit descriptions of 'disrupts', 'fights' and 'bully' to a greater extent than girls. Girls, on the other hand, have been nominated to fit descriptions of 'shy', 'seeks help' and 'victim of bullying' to a greater extent than boys (Nabuzoka and Smith, 1993). The pattern of behaviours for girls is similar to that of children with LD as a whole, but, unlike children with LD overall, girls tended to be seen as co-operative as well. However, Nabuzoka and Smith found no sex differences in status-group composition. Other studies (e.g. Bryan, 1974b, 1976; Kistner and Gatlin, 1989), found girls with LD to have lower sociometric status than boys with LD. It is possible that lower sociometric status of girls could be masked when the children are allowed to nominate peers of any gender for the status categories. In this way, boys' nominations of girls with LD would be less negative than those of fellow girls who would be aware of greater deviance from female peer group norms.

Nabuzoka and Smith also observed gender differences on the bully–victim dimension across the two diagnostic groups. The findings indicated that, while children with LD generally tended to be victims of bullying, girls with LD seemed particularly at risk compared to boys with LD. Also, although non-LD girls were found to be low on bullying, girls with LD were as likely to be bullies themselves as boys with LD. These girls with LD, often both victims of bullying and bullies themselves, are likely to be 'provocative victims'.

The reasons why girls with LD should be more at risk in this way are not clear. It is generally recognized, however, that children who appear to be somewhat different from peers tend to be victimized more. It is possible that since fewer girls tend to be diagnosed with LD, those who are would tend to be regarded as significantly different from their peers. It is also possible that being a bully here was simply a reaction against being bullied. These explanations of the interaction of sex and LD status in accounting for differences in sociometric status and behaviour need to be explored further in future research.

Teacher assessments of social behaviour

Teacher assessments of children's behaviour provide another way of identifying children who may have problems in social relations. There has been consistent evidence that children with LD tend to be less well regarded by teachers (Cardell and Parmar, 1988; Garrett and Crump, 1980; Merrell, 1991). In one study, Gresham and Reschly (1986) found that teachers perceived some children with LD as socially deficient in interpersonal interactions and in self-regulatory behaviour such as having positive attitudes and expressing emotions. Another study by Cardell and Parmer (1988) found that teachers rated students with LD as more withdrawn, less persistent, more distractible and less flexible than non-LD individuals.

It is likely that teacher assessments mostly reflect perceptions in classroom situations and other formal settings where academic behaviour is emphasized or at least considered. Hence, teacher assessments of social behaviour are likely to be strongly related to academic ability. However, these assessments have been found to be related also to social status of children with or without LD (Roberts and Zubrick, 1993).

Some studies have used teacher assessments to look specifically at the relationship between academic achievement and social competence as well as social adjustment. For example, Haager and Vaughn (1995) examined the social competence of students with LD, low achievement, or average-to-high achievement. Their measures included social skills, behaviour problems, peer relations and self-perceptions. Findings showed that teachers perceived students with LD and those with low achievement as demonstrating poorer social skills and more behaviour problems than average-to-high achievers. Tur-Kaspa and Bryan (1995) similarly found that teachers rated students with LD and those with low achievement as having significantly lower social competence and social adjustment than their average-achievement peers. However, this latter finding applied only to younger students (mean age 9.9 years). Teacher ratings did not discriminate those with LD, low achievement, and average achievement at the older levels (mean age 13.6 years).

These findings suggest that teacher assessments may be useful for identifying children's social problems only at certain age levels. In particular, teachers may become less aware of aspects of social behaviour related to social adjustment as the children become older and the peer group acquires greater significance. In any case, as the context of social interaction within the peer group varies from that characterized by the presence of teachers, one might expect some differences between teachers' and peer assessments. Such differences might be in the significance accorded to specific behaviours which might be characteristic of specific categories of children. The nature of interaction with children is also likely to vary as a result of different behavioural expectations.

Establishing the extent to which perceptions of teachers and those of peers are related may have implications for the design of intervention programmes that involve both teachers and peers.

The relationship between teacher and peer assessments

Teacher assessments of poorer social skills and social competence in children with LD tend to be mirrored by negative peer regard (Haager and Vaughn, 1995; Roberts and Zubrick, 1993). However, the relationship between teacher assessment of social competence and sociometric status may vary depending on the category of children being considered. For example, Haager and Vaughn found that students with LD and those with low achievement were perceived by teachers as showing poorer social skills and more behaviour problems than were students with average-to-high achievement. These students were also less liked by peers than were students with average-to-high achievement. However, only students with low achievement received significantly higher peer rejection.

It would seem that teacher assessments of behaviour may not discriminate these two groups of students whereas peer assessments of sociometric status may do so. Such differences are likely to arise if the criteria used by peers do not reflect domains covered by teacher assessments. Indeed, it is likely that teacher assessments may be influenced by perception of similar academic profiles for children with LD and children with low achievement. Peers, on the other hand, may be influenced more by non-academic social processes and reach somewhat different conclusions as to the social functioning of the two groups of children. The referent context for judging target children may be an important factor here.

Nabuzoka and Smith (1993) obtained assessments of children with LD and non-LD children from class teachers on a number of interpersonal skills covering a variety of situations. These were compared with the peer nominations on the eight behavioural descriptions described earlier. The teacher assessments were obtained using the *Social Behaviour at School Questionnaire* developed by Spence (1985). The scores derived from this questionnaire cover a wide range of behaviour across situations in the school context. The questionnaire first requires the teacher to read through a list of 42 items related to interpersonal skills. Then the teacher observes an individual child in a variety of situations until he or she feels able to answer the questions adequately and reliably, by circling 'Yes' or 'No' in response to whether each item was viewed as a problem. A social competence score is given for each item where no problem is indicated, and these are added up to yield a total (raw) score for each child.

Nabuzoka and Smith found that teachers rated non-LD children significantly more positively than children with LD. This was generally consistent with the sociometric measures obtained through peer nominations. However, they also found that the relationship between teachers' scores of social behaviour and peer nominations to various behavioural categories varied markedly. Significant correlations were found between teacher scores and peer nominations for non-LD children but not for children with LD. This would seem to suggest that while teachers and peers may both have identified children with LD as having some problems in social relations, their assessment of behaviour that would account for such status differed.

How might differences between teacher and peer assessments of the behaviour of children with LD arise? One possible explanation is that teachers *perceive and interpret* the behaviour differently. Teachers and child peers may use different criteria only when considering children with LD, but regard non-LD children similarly. This explanation is largely supported by a follow-up study, which examined the relationship between teacher ratings and peer nominations of children both with and without LD. Class teachers were asked to rate children with LD and non-LD children, including those whose peer nominations had been collected on several behavioural descriptors ('co-operates', 'disrupts', 'shy', 'starts fights', 'seeks help', 'leader', 'bully', and 'victim of bullying'). The same behavioural descriptions used by peers in an earlier study (Nabuzoka and Smith, 1993) were given to the teachers to determine whether teacher perceptions of similar behaviour differed from those of the peers.

It was found that teacher ratings and peer nominations were significantly correlated for non-LD children but not for children with LD. Both teachers and peers scored the latter higher on victim and shy behaviour and non-LD children higher on leadership and co-operative behaviours. Children who were scored highly as bullies by teachers and peers were also scored highly as disruptive and as starting fights, but scored low as co-operative by teachers. Correlation of 'victim' with 'shy' and 'help seeking' behaviours were significant for peers, but not for teachers. Thus, whereas peers regarded victims as 'shy', as well as 'seeking help', teachers did not. Instead, teachers tended to associate victims with fighting, being disruptive and being less co-operative.

These differences between teacher and peer ratings were related to the children's LD status. For example, whereas peers provided very similar correlations for children with LD and non-LD children regarding bullies and victims, teachers did not always do so. Teachers saw children involved as either bullies or as victims as uncooperative, *except* for children with LD. They also saw children with LD who were victims as not being shy. These differences could lie in the realities of the situation or were merely teachers' perceptions, but peers did not perceive them. As behaviour tends to be largely context-specific, it is likely that teachers' and peers' assessments of children's behaviour are based on, and largely reflect, the various situations and opportunities for observing the behaviours.

In the case of evaluating normally developing children's behaviour, assessment of social competence by teachers can largely be expected to be consistent with that of peers. This is because there is no reason to expect that the child's level of abilities in the general construct of social competence will vary significantly across situations. A child with adequate interpersonal skills can, for example, function adequately in the presence or absence of adults. His or her behaviour towards peers and towards adults will largely be within the child's repertoire of social skills. However, for children with LD, observed social competence may vary more across situations.

Bryan and Perlmutter (1979), for example, reported that children with LD tended to be judged as more socially competent in the presence of younger as opposed to older peers. This difference in the social functioning of children with LD was attributed to their ability to decode social environments. In this case, the situation with a younger peer was seen as easier to decode as the social role of the older child being in charge could easily be understood and therefore executed. In the presence of an older peer, on the other hand, the role of the child with LD was less clear in the light of a lack of age superiority and the child's own perceived failure in other areas, such as relative low achievement in the academic domain. Perlmutter (1986) thus suggested that problems of children with LD in peer relations may emanate not from a lack of ability to perform appropriate behaviours *per se*, but from failure to decode social situations – thereby leading to an inability to understand when it is appropriate to perform certain behaviours.

The notion that children with LD may have deficits in decoding social environments is a plausible explanation for the lack of correlation between peer and teacher assessments. The few opportunities teachers have to observe children's behaviour are in the classroom. Such situations are relatively easy for the children to decode, as the social roles are clearly defined. Peers, on the other hand, have opportunities to observe children with LD in relatively unstructured situations where teachers may not be present. The demands of such situations may not be so easy for children with LD to decode. For example, as we saw in Chapter 4, rough-and-tumble play presents cues that may be difficult to decode because it resembles real fighting. Resultant inappropriate responses by children with LD can lead to peer assessments that are less positive than teacher assessments.

Similarly, a child could also be constantly picked on as a victim of bullying simply because he or she has not managed to understand how to avoid being victimized. In addition, such a child might frequently react aggressively and thus be perceived as a 'provocative victim'. Peers who base their assessment of the behaviour of a child with LD in such situations arrive at a different conclusion from that of teachers. It has been reported, for example, that teachers often do not notice how much bullying is going on in their school (Whitney and Smith, 1993).

The behavioural attributes of children with LD that have implications for their social relations therefore seem to be influenced by underlying social perceptual and cognitive abilities of the children. This is consistent with a hypothesized relationship between social cognitive functioning and behaviour (see Chapters 3 and 4).

Social behaviour and social adjustment

The relationship between some behavioural attributes of children with LD and their sociometric status, reported by Nabuzoka and Smith (1993), is further illustrated in the study by Rønning and Nabuzoka

(1993). A group of children with LD (defined as having mild-to-moderate intellectual disabilities) aged 8–12 years participated in a series of interventions that were applied at intervals separated by baselines. These interventions included social skills training, play skills training and prompting, and a 'special friends' intervention. Observations of behaviour were made and recorded in terms of 'negative' or 'positive' initiations and social interactions. Assessments of sociometric status were carried out at three points: at the end of the first baseline, during the baseline following social skills training and prompting, and finally during the first follow-up following the 'special friends' training. Thus, it was expected that if sociometric status was related to social behaviour, any changes in 'negative' or 'positive' behaviour should be associated with corresponding changes in the sociometric status of the children.

Initial baseline observations of behaviour showed low levels of positive interaction between children with LD and peers. Social skills training of the children with LD led to some increases in interaction between the two groups of children, but training coupled with prompts led to more substantial increases. The 'special friends' intervention led to even more increases in positive social interaction. In all cases, increases in positive interaction were characterized by increases in appropriate initiations and responses by children with LD. In addition, increases were observed in positive sociometric ratings of children with LD by their non-LD peers. These increases in sociometric status corresponded with the intervention programmes and conformed with increases in positive behaviours and interactions. Overall, positive behavioural initiations and responses of children with LD were associated with positive status and acceptance as indicated by increased positive social interaction. This suggests a strong link between behaviour and social adjustment of children with LD.

Finally, one main aim of intervention approaches is to develop positive social interaction and thereby integration of children with LD. As the study by Rønning and Nabuzoka (1993) indicated, establishing levels of both 'negative' and 'positive' behaviours among the target children is important as the former can then be discouraged while encouraging the latter. However, while research has focused mainly on behaviours associated with maladjustment, differences between children with LD and non-LD children regarding desirable social behaviours are much less clear. Some studies have not found any differences between groups on positive behaviours (Bryan *et al.*, 1976), while others have suggested that children with LD display more positive social behaviour than do non-LD peers (Bryan, 1978).

It is probable that these and other conflicting findings reflect methodological differences (discussed in Chapter 7). However, it would appear that future research should not be concerned just with the extent to which children with LD may be characterized by negative or positive behaviours. A lot more needs to be done to identify approaches that not only promote 'appropriate' behaviour but also impart social cognitive skills that enable the children to understand when certain behaviours are inappropriate.

Summary and conclusions

Research generally indicates a relationship between some behavioural attributes and the sociometric status of children with or without LD. Some patterns of attributes distinguish these two groups of children, and could explain differences in sociometric status. Research also indicates that the nature and/or quality of behaviour of children with LD may vary across situations, depending on particular social cognitive demands. Thus, some children with LD may behave competently in uncomplicated situations with clearly defined roles, but behave less competently in complex and ambiguous situations.

These findings together seem to indicate that problems faced by some children with LD in peer relations may not emanate solely from a lack of ability to behave appropriately in general terms, but rather from their inability to understand the demands of certain situations. The children may have appropriate skills in their behavioural repertoire, but lack the ability to recognize when to apply them. In this sense social cognitive difficulties may be implicated in the behavioural characteristics of some children with LD, which are associated with adjustment problems.

Therefore one task for clinicians, educators and researchers is to identify which children lack appropriate behavioural skills and which possess the skills but lack the requisite social cognitive abilities. Perlmutter (1986) suggested that the majority of children with LD are in the latter category, accounting largely for their problems in social relations. Remedial programmes focusing on teaching specific behaviours to such children in a bid to develop social abilities were therefore seen to be inappropriate. Instead, it was suggested that more attention should be paid to the social environment and why those behaviours might be appropriate given the complete social context of interaction.

A similar point was made in Chapter 3 regarding social perceptual abilities. Being able to identify specific social cues, or to execute certain behavioural responses, may be useful. However, it would appear that for children with LD to interact successfully with others it is important for them also to understand various contexts of social interaction. Training children with LD in such social understanding would better prepare them to respond appropriately to others. Such training could include the skill of being able to decode situational determinants of other people's disposition, and matching their own responses to the demands of the situation.

Chapter 6

Social cognition, behaviour and social adjustment

This chapter further examines, and provides an integration of, some findings on the relationship between various aspects of the model of social functioning and adjustment of children with LD presented in Chapter 1. According to the model (refer to Figure 1.2), behavioural attributes of children with LD reflect their social cognitive functioning and account for the nature and quality of their social relations. Data are presented from studies that have sought and provided empirical evidence for the linkages in the model. In this chapter, *social cognitive measures* include both the perception and processing of social information by the child. *Behavioural dispositions* relate to the child's characteristic ways of behaving towards others. *Social adjustment* relates to the quality of social relations experienced by the child.

Dimensions of social functioning and adjustment

Interrelationships between various dimensions of social functioning and adjustment, as considered in the studies reviewed in preceding chapters, can be depicted as shown in Figure 6.1. This represents an elaboration of the social cognitive model of adjustment presented in Figure 1.2. The structure is basically a relationship between social cognition, social behaviour and social adaptation. This holds true if we use the social cognitive model of information processing proposed by Dodge *et al.* (1986) and consider social perception as constituting the encoding step of the model, judgement of peer behaviour as the step of interpretation, and perceived behaviour as the end result (enactment) arising from processing of the social information. Social adjustment in this case constitutes an overall measure of the quality of peer relations as measured by the child's sociometric status and teacher assessment, as well as the subjective social emotional experiences of the child.

In Figure 6.1, linkages depicted by arrows represent a hypothezised relationship between social cognition, social behaviour and social adjustment in which the preceding dimension is a precursor to one that

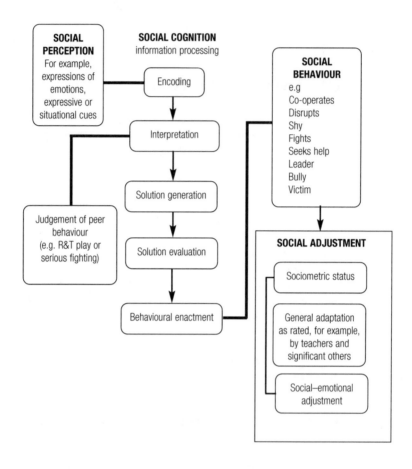

Figure 6.1 *Structure of relations between social cognitive functioning (including social perception), social behaviour and social adjustment*

immediately follows. Aspects of social functioning corresponding to each other are merely linked accordingly. In determining the utility of the model, there is a need to discover empirical linkages between variables that are said to be linked within dimensions, as well as linkages across dimensions. Findings from studies that have been reviewed in previous chapters indicate some support for such linkages. The data presented in this chapter further illustrates the nature and strength of the linkages by identifying some specific variables.

As we saw in Chapters 3 and 4, a number of studies have indicated that children with LD are developmentally less advanced in social cognitive skills (including social perception) than other children of similar chronological age. Given that these children also experience proportionally more social adjustment problems than peers, a number of relationships supporting the model in Figure 6.1 are hypothezised. Specifically, if the social perceptual and social cognitive abilities of children with LD are related to social adjustment, social adjustment measures such as sociometric status should be correlated with performance on various aspects of social cognitive functioning. Given a relationship between sociometric status and behavioural attributes (indicated in Chapter 5), social perceptual and cognitive abilities of children with LD should also be correlated with social behaviour.

What evidence do we have for any of these relationships? Some studies have provided data on children with LD indicating links within specific dimensions such as the social cognitive dimension of information processing (Gomez and Hazeldine, 1996; Tur-Kaspa and Bryan, 1994), and between some dimensions such as social cognition and behaviour (Kravetz *et al.*, 1999), and between social behaviour and social adjustment (Nabuzoka and Smith, 1993). However, such studies have focused only on some aspects of the model without providing data on all dimensions.

One of the few studies that have provided data on almost all aspects of the model was reported by Nabuzoka (1993). In this chapter, data from that study is presented and discussed together with some findings from other relevant studies that have a bearing on the model. First, data are presented on the nature of links between social perceptual and social information processing measures. The next concern is with the extent and nature of the relationship between these measures and the children's social behaviours in various contexts. Then, data are presented and examined regarding the extent to which those behaviours of children with LD can account for their quality of peer relationships. These data thus provide an empirical basis for evaluating the validity of the suggested relationship between social cognitive functioning and behaviour of children with LD, and between behaviour and the quality of social relations experienced.

Measures of social perception and social information processing

We saw in Chapter 3 that children with LD can be distinguished from non-LD peers on social perceptual abilities. Children with LD generally tend to be less accurate than non-LD children on tasks involving such abilities. The data bearing on this were provided in the report by Nabuzoka and Smith (1995) and were depicted in Figure 3.1. The findings regarding children's resolution of conflicting cues, and reliance on

situational rather than expressive cues, suggest developmental progression associated with social cognitive abilities. In Chapter 4, we saw
that the children's ability to distinguish rough-and-tumble play from
real fighting indicated developmental differentiation on cue interpretation among children with LD, as well as relative to non-LD children.
A relationship between the ability to make an overall judgement of a
behavioural episode and identification of a variety of social cues was
also observed. These findings were reported in a recent study by
Nabuzoka and Smith (1999) and together they suggest a relationship
between social perceptual and social cognitive abilities.

The relationship between measures of social perception and social
information processing was more extensively examined in Nabuzoka
(1993). In that study, social perception measures involved identification of facial expressions, gestures and postures, and were obtained
following the procedure later described by Nabuzoka and Smith
(1995). Social information processing measures were based on the
study by Dodge *et al.* (1986), and included measures on encoding of
cues, interpretation, solution generation, solution evaluation and
behavioural enactment (see Chapter 4 for details). Regression analyses
were conducted to evaluate the predictability of competence at each of
the social information processing steps from (a) performance on identification of expressive cues (facial expressions and postures), and (b)
relative reliance on expressive and situational cues. In addition, correlations were computed between the children's performances on the
various steps of social information processing, and on recognition of
expressive cues as well as the relative reliance on expressive and situational cues.

Analyses both for children with LD and non-LD children indicated
that significant proportions of the variance at each of the processing
steps could be accounted for by the children's social perceptual abilities (ranges $R^2 = .10$ to $R^2 = .36$, $p < .04$ to $p < .001$). For example,
identification of expressive cues were significantly correlated with
each of the information processing steps ($p < .05$ to $p < .001$), except for
that between facial expressions and response evaluation. For children
with LD, identification of facial expressions was significantly correlated with encoding of available cues ($r = .38$, $p < .01$), interpretation of
available cues in rough-and-tumble episodes ($r = .45$, $p < .001$), and
enactment of an appropriate response in the peer group entry situation
($r = .37$, $p < .01$). Identification of postures was significantly correlated
with all the social information processing steps of encoding ($r = .42$,
$p < .001$), interpretation of rough-and-tumble cues ($r = .60$, $p < .001$),
solution generation ($r = .30$, $p < .01$), evaluation of possible solutions
($r = .36$, $p < .01$) and behavioural enactment ($r = .49$, $p < .001$).

Correlations were also established between scores of children with
LD on various aspects of situational and expressive cues on the one
hand, and on social information processing variables. Performance on

interpretation of social cues (rough-and-tumble episodes) was correlated with reliance on expressions when congruent with situational cues ($r = .49, p < .01$). The correlation with reliance on situational cues in such cases was negative ($r = -.48, p < .01$). Generation of a wide range of response solutions was correlated with identification of congruent cues ($r = .33, p < .03$), and reliance on situational cues ($r = .38, p < .01$) when congruent with the expressions, and with reliance on expressions when situational and expressive cues were conflicting ($r = .29, p < .05$). Generation of potential responses was, however, negatively correlated with identification of situational cues in the presence of neutral expressions ($r = -.32, p < .05$). Accurate evaluation of potential responses was significantly correlated with identification of expressive cues in the absence of situational cues ($r = .37, p < .03$), and negatively correlated with mere identification of situational and expressive cues when they were conflicting ($r = -.30, p < .05$). Enactment of appropriate behavioural responses was correlated with identification of expressive cues in neutral situations ($r = .39, p < .01$), identification of cues when situations and expressions were congruent ($r = .31, p < .05$), and reliance on expressions in such cases ($r = .31, p < .05$).

In general terms, these analyses indicated that the children's level of social perceptual skills was linked to their social cognitive abilities. These data suggest that specific social perceptual abilities are associated with each of the information processing steps. In particular:

- accurate interpretation of social cues was mostly related to identification of expressive cues;
- generation of a wider range of solutions was associated with reliance on situational cues so long as they did not conflict with expressive cues;
- accurate evaluation of potential responses and enactment of responses was associated with identification of expressive cues.

Overall, there appears to be greater reliance on expressive than situational cues among children with LD when processing social information.

Having established some links between social perceptual and information processing measures, the next concern is with the extent and nature of the relationship between these measures and the children's social behaviours in various contexts.

Social cognitive functioning and behaviour

Social cognitive functioning as considered here includes measures of both social perception and social cognition. Measures of social perception included in the study reviewed here relate to identification of expressive cues such as facial expressions, postures and gestures (introduced in Chapter 3, and used by Nabuzoka and Smith, 1995) and contextual or situational cues (separately, and consistent or conflicting with expressive cues). Measures of social cognition include social information processing measures outlined in Chapter 4. They include: encoding, interpretation, response search, response evaluation, and enactment. Behavioural measures include peer nominations and teacher scores on general social behaviours discussed in Chapter 5. These nominations were obtained on the following behaviours: 'leader', 'co-operates', 'shy', 'starts fights', 'disrupts', 'seeks help', 'bully', and 'victim'. Teacher scores represented a measure of general social competence from assessments as to the presence or absence of social problems for each child (from Spence, 1985). The higher the score, the more positive the teacher assessment.

Social perception and behaviour

Nabuzoka (1993) obtained scores on children with LD and non-LD children on social perceptual measures, peer behavioural nominations and teacher ratings of social behaviour. Analyses of correlation were then computed between variables representing these measures. Findings indicated that social perceptual abilities were significantly correlated with some peer behavioural nominations.

Being perceived as shy was negatively correlated with accuracy in identifying gesture cues ($r = -.32$, $p < .05$). That is, those children nominated by most peers as being shy were less likely to be accurate in identifying gesture cues. Seeking help was associated with identification of posture cues ($r = .37$, $p < .05$), identification of situational cues in the absence of expressive cues ($r = .53$, $p < .01$), and reliance on expressive cues when both expressive and situational cues were available ($r = .40$, $p < .05$). Nomination as a leader was associated with reliance on situational cues when they were conflicting with expressive cues ($r = .36$, $p < .05$). Nominations as victims of bullying were associated with accuracy in identifying situational cues when expressions were neutral ($r = .34$, $p < .05$), and when no expressive cues were available ($r = .35$, $p < .05$). These behavioural attributes of 'shy', 'seeks help', 'victim' and 'leader' have been found to discriminate children with LD from non-LD children (Nabuzoka and Smith, 1993; see Chapter 5).

Children scoring highly on a variety of social behaviours as assessed by teachers were also more likely to rely on the expressive cues of postures ($r = .38$, $p < .05$), and less on situational cues when they were congruent with expressive cues ($r = .29$, $p < .05$). In addition, these children were less likely to resolve conflicting situational and expressive cues ($r = -.59$, $p < .01$). However, it was observed that it was the combination of variables that accounted for a child's level of social competence from the teachers' point of view. For example, regression analyses indicated that reliance on situational or expressive cues, identification and resolution of conflicting situational and expressive cues accounted for a significant proportion of teacher scores of social behaviour (R^2 = .26, p < .05). Resolution of conflicting situational and expressive cues accounted for 29% of variance in teacher scores of behaviour (p < .01).

To summarize, social perceptual skills involving identification of expressive and situational cues were associated with behavioural nominations that have been shown to discriminate children with LD from non-LD peers (i.e. 'shy', 'seeks help', 'victim', and 'leader'). Those children nominated as being shy by peers were less likely to identify gesture cues. The children nominated as seeking help were likely to be adept at identification of postural cues, to identify situational cues in the absence of expressive cues, but likely to rely on expressive cues when both expressive and situational cues were available. Reliance on situational cues when conflicting with expressive cues was associated with being nominated as a leader. Those nominated as victims of bullying were more likely to identify situational cues only when expressions were neutral, and also when no expressive cues were available. For teachers, on the other hand, children adept at a variety of social behaviours were more likely to rely on expressive cues, and less on situational cues when they were congruent with expressive cues. In addition, those children were also less likely to resolve conflicting situational and expressive cues.

However, it was the combination of variables that accounted for a child's level of social competence as assessed by teachers. For example, reliance on situational or expressive cues, identification, and resolution of conflicting situational and expressive cues accounted for a significant proportion of teacher scores of social behaviour. This would be consistent with the fact that teacher assessments covered a wide range of social behaviours in various situations.

Social information processing and behaviour

As we saw earlier in this chapter, various measures of social perception correlate significantly with a number of measures of social cognitive abilities of information processing. Indeed, some may argue, social perception can be considered to be an aspect of social cognitive functioning essentially concerned with the encoding step of social information processing (see Figure 6.1). Thus children adept at perception of social cues in effect exhibit aspects of social cognitive skills. In addition, various steps of social information processing tend to be intercorrelated (see Chapter 4). But the nature of correlational relationships is such that one cannot determine the direction of that relationship, or indeed whether or not it is a causal one. In this respect, and though significant proportions of social cognitive abilities could be predicted from social perceptual abilities, inferences on the relationship between social cognition and behaviour cannot be made on the basis of the relationship between social perception and behaviour. Bearing this in mind, it is necessary to examine some empirical studies on the relationship between social information processing measures and social behaviour of children with LD.

Nabuzoka (1993) also examined the relationship between social cognitive measures of information processing, including interpretation of peer group behaviour, and the behaviour of children with LD as perceived by peers and teachers. Significant but negative correlations were found between the processing step of behavioural enactment (self-report and role-play) and peer nominations of children with LD as 'co-operative' ($r = -.32$, $p < .05$), 'shy' ($r = -.29$, $p < .05$) and 'leader' ($r = -.40$, $p < .01$). Interpretation of social cues (using rough-and-tumble video episodes) was positively correlated with nominations as one who 'starts fights' ($r = .36$, $p < .05$), and negatively correlated with being seen as a 'victim' of bullying ($r = -.36$, $p < .05$). Regression analyses indicated that 18% of variance in nominations as a leader were accounted for by all the processing variables of encoding, interpreting, response search, evaluation and enactment, but this only approached significance ($R = .56$, $p < .06$). The two variables of response evaluation and behavioural enactment, however, accounted for a significant variance (22%) of nominations as leader ($R = .52$, $p < .01$). This pattern of findings suggests that, while perception of leadership qualities in children with LD by peers may be related to the overall social cognitive abilities of the former, peer perceptions of such behaviour as being co-operative, being shy and showing leadership may not necessarily reflect understanding of appropriate behaviours by children with LD.

Teacher assessments of social behaviour were also analysed in relation to social cognitive variables. Results indicated significant correlations of teacher scores of social behaviour (general competence) with encoding or identification of available cues ($r = .23$, $p < .05$), and enactment of an optimal behavioural response. Regression analyses indicated that the information processing variables of identification of present cues, interpretation and behavioural enactment accounted for a significant proportion (13%) of the variance in teacher scores ($R = .36$, $p < .05$). Overall, it was observed that a combination of skills at various steps of information processing accounted for much of the children's level of social functioning as assessed by teachers, perhaps underlining the general nature of the skills being assessed. Children assessed to frequently engage in appropriate social behaviours by their class teachers were also adept at identification of available cues, at their interpretation, and at enacting appropriate behavioural responses to the peer group entry situation. Peer nominations, on the other hand, indicated that while those children considered to be shy by peers were less likely to enact appropriate behavioural responses, those considered to be co-operative and/or possessing leadership qualities were also less likely to enact an appropriate behavioural response to the peer group entry situation.

Two considerations can be made in interpreting these findings. First, class teachers and the children may have differed in their conception of what constitutes desirable behaviour. In this case, being one who is perceived as co-operative or a leader according to peer group norms might not necessarily be one who engages in appropriate behaviours by adult standards. Behavioural enactment was scored in terms of appropriateness as judged by an adult assessor (see Chapter 4 for a description of the procedure) and perhaps much more likely to correspond to that of other adults such as teachers. In addition, children with LD may be treated differently (from non-LD children) by their peers, such that the criteria for evaluating various behavioural attributes of these children would be different relative to non-LD peers. Furthermore, it is possible that the measure of behavioural enactment may not have adequately captured the range of these children's behavioural skills. This may have included behaviour deemed by peers to be uncooperative or lacking in leadership qualities.

Second, only the variables of cue interpretation and behavioural enactment were significantly correlated with peer behavioural nominations in the study by Nabuzoka (1993). This would indicate that only these two processing steps may be associated with behaviour as judged by peers. These two variables were associated with peer behavioural nominations including 'leader', 'co-operates', 'shy', 'starts fights', and 'victim'. The variable of behavioural enactment should, by definition, have a direct correspondence with behavioural predisposition. However, as we have just seen, ability to enact appropriate behaviour by children with LD may not necessarily correspond to peer evaluation of the same in terms of other behavioural categories. Thus, the finding that those children seen as shy were also likely to be less adept at behavioural enactment would have been expected given that shy behaviour could be associated with vulnerability. On the other hand, the relationship between ability to enact appropriate behaviour and being perceived by peers as less co-operative or meeting the criteria of a leader may indicate differential peer perceptions of children with LD as regards contextually relevant behaviour.

The variable of cue interpretation, unlike that of behavioural enactment, can be regarded as a core cognitive function whose relationship to behavioural dispositions may reflect a different form of interaction with contextual factors. For example, the pattern of behaviour related to cue interpretation could be explained in relation to experiences of bullying and victimization by children with LD. Cue interpretation was associated with 'starts fights' and 'victim': those children adept at cue interpretation tended to be seen as starting fights, while those who were seen as victims of bullying tended to be less adept at cue interpretation (Nabuzoka, 1993). It has been documented that children with LD experience proportionally more bullying and victimization than non-LD peers. It is possible that some of the children may react to such experiences, for example by starting fights, to offset the bullying behaviour. These children may thus correctly interpret their vulnerable status of being likely to be picked on (scoring highly on cue interpretation). On the other hand, those children frequently victimized may not often accurately interpret the circumstances that put them at risk for peer victimization, this being reflected in their scoring low on cue interpretation. Such an explanation is consistent with the findings by Sutton *et al.* (1999) regarding social cognitive abilities of children who are bullies. According to Sutton and colleagues, some children involved in bullying others may use this behaviour for their own ends (e.g. to avoid being bullied themselves), thereby having more cognitive sophistication than they have often been credited with.

In conclusion, there is some evidence for significant relationships between social information processing steps and behaviour of children with LD. Those steps to do with perception of relevant cues, interpretation, and enactment are associated with peer behavioural nominations, including those that have been shown to discriminate children with LD from non-LD children. In addition, these processing steps together may account for general social competence as assessed by teachers.

Having established the relationship between social perception and social information processing variables, and between social perception and some behaviours, the picture that emerges is that of a link between behaviour and social cognitive functioning. Conceptually, social cognitive functioning and social behaviour constitute elements of overall social functioning considered to be social skills. We saw in Chapter 5 that certain patterns of behaviour can be associated with sociometric status, which is an aspect of social adjustment. This suggests significant correlations between various measures of social functioning and social adjustment measures. This will now be examined further.

Social functioning and social adjustment

It was pointed out in Chapter 1 that measures of social functioning include cognitive and behavioural skills, the evaluation of which constitute the level of social competence for a given child. Social adjustment, as discussed in this section, needs to be operationalized once more.

Social adjustment for children with LD in integrated settings can be said to refer to how well these children fit into the overall school context, both in terms of personal experiences and as perceived by others. It refers to the quality of social relations experienced by a particular child and may include their sociometric position in a group of other children, as well as their socio-emotional experiences. In the context of peer relations in integrated settings, social adjustment as measured by sociometric status may be taken to particularly refer to the extent to which non-LD peers socially accept children with LD. It can partly be measured by how well a particular child is liked by peers. Such acceptance by peers is moderated by the degree to which the child is disliked (yielding an index of social preference), or the influence exerted by the child on his or her peers as a result of being liked *and* disliked (social impact). Social adjustment can also be determined using assessments made by significant adults such as teachers, and even direct observations of interaction patterns. Information regarding personal socio-emotional experiences of the children themselves adds another dimension to assessment of social adjustment.

This section will focus on measures of social adjustment related to peer relations, including peer perceptions and teacher assessments. Findings suggesting that children with LD are less liked by normally developing peers, and are recipients of more negative social experiences in integrated settings, indicate that children with LD are less well adjusted in such settings. The main concern is to determine whether direct relationships exist between these measures of social adjustment and social cognitive and behavioural aspects of social functioning.

First, data linking behaviour and social adjustment of children with LD are examined, followed by the relationship between social cognitive measures involving social perception and information processing, and measures of social adjustment.

Behaviour and social adjustment

Data illustrating the relationship between behaviour and the social adjustment measures related to sociometric status are presented from Nabuzoka (1993). The first analyses focus on measures of sociometric status across which behavioural attributes as perceived by peers were compared. As we saw in Chapter 5, some patterns of behaviour are associated with some categories of sociometric status (Nabuzoka and Smith, 1993). However, sociometric status measures embody positive (i.e. 'like most') and negative ('like least') scores which both contribute to 'social preference' and 'social impact' measures. Such measures are useful in gauging a balanced view of the status of children among peers. However, they may also mask the strength of relationship with measures of social functioning. For this reason, the scores of children with LD and non-LD children on 'like most' and 'like least' nominations, as well as social impact and social preference scores, were separately analysed as direct indices of social adjustment (Nabuzoka, 1993; Nabuzoka and Smith, 1993).

Findings indicated that non-LD children were liked significantly more than children with LD ($p < .05$). Children with LD, on the other hand, were disliked significantly more than non-LD children ($p < .05$). Similar analyses of social preference indicated that non-LD children were more positively regarded than children with LD ($p < .01$). The two groups of children did not differ on social impact, a finding which is not surprising as this measure retains both negative and positive nominations in the final score.

The second concern is to relate social adjustment to perceived behaviour of these children. If the level of social adjustment of children with LD is related to their behaviour, we should find a relationship between various behavioural attributes and those measures reflecting acceptance. Again, research findings indicate this to be the case (Nabuzoka and Smith, 1993). Further regression analysis of the data indicated that various behavioural attributes ('co-operates', 'disrupts', 'shy', 'fights', 'seeks help', 'leader', bully', and 'victim') accounted for significant variance (24%) of nominations as liked most by peers ($R = .64, p < .05$), and also accounted for significant variance (48%) of being liked least by peers ($R = .77, p < .001$). In addition, all the behavioural nominations taken together accounted for significant variance (32%) of social impact scores ($R = .69, p < .05$) but not of social preference.

Since concern at this stage is to determine the patterns of behaviour associated with negative social adjustment of children with LD, negative social behaviours would be the prime suspects. For children with LD, the three behavioural nominations of 'disrupts', 'fights', and 'bully' accounted for a significant amount of the variance (27%) in social preference scores ($R = .57, p < .01$) and another significant amount of variance (22%) in social impact scores ($R = .54, p < .01$). The three behavioural nominations of 'shy', 'seeks help' and 'victim', where children with LD scored higher than non-LD children, were not significantly predictive of social impact (accounting for only 8% of the variance) or social preference (accounting for less than 2% of the variance). For non-LD children, the three behavioural nominations of 'disrupts', 'fights' and 'bully' accounted for a significant amount of the variance (30%) of social preference scores ($R = .56, p < .001$) and also a significant amount of variance (11%) of social impact scores ($R = .36, p < .001$). The behavioural nominations of 'shy', 'seeks help' and 'victim' also accounted for significant amount of variance (35%) in social preference scores ($R = .61, p < .0001$) and a smaller but statistically significant amount of variance (4%) in social impact scores ($R = .25, p < .05$). Nominations on behaviours of 'leader' and 'co-operates', where children with LD scored lower than non-LD children, were not predictive of social impact or social preference for children with LD. For non-LD children, the two behavioural nominations of 'leader' and 'co-operates' accounted for a significant amount of variance (13%) in social impact scores ($R = .38$, $p < .001$), and also a significant amount of variance (33%) of social preference scores ($R = .58$, $p < .001$).

To illustrate the relationship between popularity (liked or disliked) and behavioural attributes, a simple cluster analysis (SCLA) indicating significant intercorrelations among variables (McQuitty, 1957), was made separately for children with LD and non-LD children (Figure 6.2). While the patterns of behaviour related to being liked were simi-

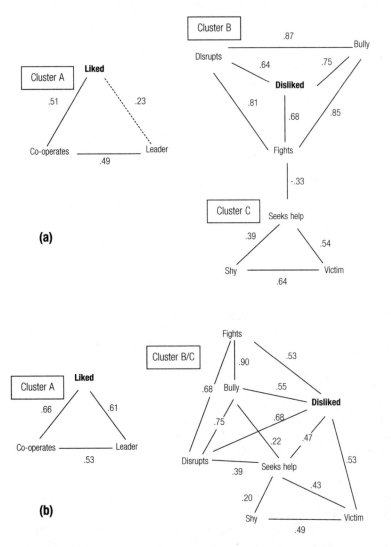

Figure 6.2 *Cluster linkage of behavioural nominations by peers with 'like' and 'dislike' nominations for (a) children with LD and (b) non-LD children*

lar for children with LD and those without, differences were observed with regard to patterns of behaviour associated with being disliked.

Being liked by peers for children both with and without LD was associated with the cluster of attributes of 'co-operates' and 'leader' (*cluster A*). For children with LD, being disliked was associated with the cluster of attributes of 'disrupts', 'fights' and 'bully' (*cluster B*). A related cluster included attributes of 'seeks help', 'shy' and 'victim (of bullying)' (*cluster C*). For non-LD children, being disliked was associated, similar to children with LD, with attributes of 'disrupts', 'fights' and 'bully', but this cluster also included attributes of 'seeks help', 'shy', and 'victim' (*cluster B/C*).

This picture of patterns of behaviour for children with LD relative to that for non-LD children suggests that the behavioural attributes for cluster C are a distinguishing feature between the two groups of children. In particular, the lack of a direct relationship between the social adjustment dimension of cluster B and cluster C for children with LD, specifically between any variable of cluster C and being disliked, suggests that the relationship of behavioural attributes of 'seeks help', 'shy' and 'victim' to social adjustment as measured by the degree of being liked or disliked is different for LD and non-LD children.

These findings indicate that, while the behaviours considered here may contribute to non-LD children's impact or effect on their peers, and also to their overall level of adjustment (social preference), the level of social acceptance (and hence social adjustment) of children with LD cannot be fully accounted for by these behavioural attributes. For these children, therefore, it may be other characteristics significantly associated with the 'like least' variable, and which distinguish them from non-LD children, that may account for their overall social adjustment (e.g. social preference). Such attributes – behavioural or otherwise – have not been identified in the studies so far considered. The behaviours of 'seeks help', 'shy' and 'victim' distinguish LD from non-LD children, but they are not significantly associated with these children being liked least. Thus, social adjustment (as measured by social preference) may also be influenced by other variables than just the behaviours being considered.

If we speculate on children's peer group norms, it may be, for instance, that evaluations by peers reflecting social adjustment may have been mediated by considerations that were context-specific. For example, the need for help of children perceived to be incapable of fighting for themselves in the context of peer group conflict could be reason to dislike them. This could explain a negative correlation, with fighting behaviour being the link for disliking children with LD ($r = -.33$). The need for measures to be context-specific is one methodological concern discussed earlier in the context of social understanding. This point is discussed further in Chapter 7 in relation to the validity of sociometric measures based on peer nominations.

Social perception and adjustment

In relating identification of expressive cues to social adjustment, Nabu-zoka (1993) found that only the identification of facial expressions was significantly associated with fewer peer nominations of 'liked most' ($r = -.30, p < .05$). Three variables of identification of facial expressions, postures and gestures were not predictive of social preference, social impact, 'like most' nominations nor 'like least' nominations. In addition, nominations for 'like least' did not indicate any significant correlation with any measure of social perception when reliance on expressive cues was compared with reliance on situational cues. 'Like most' nominations were, however, negatively correlated with reliance on expressive cues in neutral situations ($r = -41, p < .05$), and positively with reliance on situations consistent with expressive cues ($r = .40, p < .05$). A negative correlation between reliance on expressions, when situational and expressive cues were available, and 'like most' nominations was also observed ($r = -.37, p < .05$). There was a similar correlation of 'like most' nominations with reliance on expressive cues in the absence of situational cues.

Overall, the combined effects of the ability to identify expressive cues did not account for significant proportions of any of the social adjustment variables individually. However, 'like most' nominations were associated with less reliance on expressive cues, but more on situational cues. Thus, children who were liked most by peers tended to rely more on situational cues than expressive cues. As reliance on situational rather than expressive cues is associated with greater social cognitive advancement, we can conclude that children who were popular among peers (with positive social adjustment) were also likely to show greater competence on social perceptual skills.

Social cognition and adjustment

Nabuzoka (1993) found that, apart from the correlation between the social cognitive dimension of behavioural enactment (self-report and role-play) and 'like most' nominations ($r = -.32, p < .05$), no other social cognitive measure was significantly associated with social adjustment. That there was this relationship is consistent with the findings on correlation between social behaviour and sociometric status as behavioural enactment relates to social behaviour. The direction of this relationship, as discussed earlier, could reflect differences in criteria of scoring appropriate behavioural enactment by the adult researcher when compared with peer criteria for 'like most' nominations.

A general lack of relationship between various social cognitive measures and sociometric measures is consistent with the findings on the relations between social perception and adjustment. These findings together are consistent with the observations made in Chapter 4. As we saw, social cognitive functioning may not accurately predict social adjustment as measured by sociometric status, for a number of reasons. For example, both high and lower functioning individuals could have similar status, such as being disliked for different reasons. In addition, problems in social cognitive functioning may relate to specific contexts and situations (such as those that are ambiguous). As such functioning may influence behaviour on which sociometric assessments may be based, social cognitive functioning in one context may not necessarily be correlated with sociometric measures which are likely to be based on behaviour in a wider range of situations. The social cognitive measures in the study reviewed here related specifically to a peer group entry situation. It is likely that skills associated with such a task may not have captured the range and breadth of skills in areas on which peers judged children with LD for sociometric status.

Linking social cognition, behaviour and social adjustment

What then, is the overall picture of the relationship between social functioning and social adjustment of children with LD? First, various measures of social perception were significantly related to various steps of social information processing. Some social cognitive skills were also significantly related to behavioural attributes that have been identified to distinguish children with LD from non-LD children. Various social perceptual measures were predictive of positive assessments by teachers on general social competence. There was also some evidence of a significant relationship between social cognitive steps of information processing and the behaviour of children with LD as judged by peers and teachers. The social cognitive skills of perception of relevant cues, interpretation, and enactment were also associated with peer behavioural nominations shown to discriminate children with LD from non-LD children. In addition, these processing steps together were predictive of general social competence as assessed by teachers. Thus, there is some evidence for a link between social cognitive functioning and behaviour of children with LD.

Second, examination of the relationship between behaviour and social adjustment indicates that, while the patterns of behaviour associated with positive status (being liked by peers) are similar for children with LD and non-LD children, those associated with negative status (rejected or neglected) are different for the two groups. However, while children with LD tend to be less liked and more disliked than non-LD children, the specific clusters of behaviour that distinguish these two groups of children may not necessarily be associated with unpopularity for children with LD. This finding suggests that other variables may be associated with such children being less well socially adjusted, either separately or as mediator variables. It is also likely that it is the interaction of variables that may be significantly related to the social adjustment of children with LD.

Third, there is a general lack of direct links between various social perception and social cognition variables with social adjustment. Thus, the ability to identify expressive cues was not predictive of the social adjustment variables. However, 'like most' nominations were associated with less reliance on expressive cues, but more on situational cues. This suggests that children who are liked most by peers tend to rely more on situational cues than expressive cues. As this reliance may indicate higher cognitive functioning, it suggests that cognitive functioning may nonetheless be implicated in social adjustment of children with LD. However, the relationship between specific aspects of social cognitive functioning and social adjustment is likely to depend on a number of factors. Some of these relate to the context and content of the situation within which such functioning is assessed.

Can we say conclusively that the social functioning of children with LD is significantly implicated in the nature of their social adjustment? Research indicates that children with LD tend to be less accurate in perception of social cues than non-LD peers. However, there is also some evidence that the social perceptual skills of children with LD improve with age, even though they may not reach the same levels as those of non-LD peers (Jackson *et al.*, 1987; Nabuzoka and Smith, 1995). There is some evidence that children with LD also have less developed social cognitive skills as relates to analysis or processing of social infor- mation (Tur-Kaspa and Bryan, 1994). Theoretically, such limitations would explain the tone of their interpersonal interactions as an indi- vidual's appraisal and understanding of situations informs behaviour. Thus, inability to interpret subtle body language cues (Sisterhen and Gerber, 1989) could explain why the interpersonal interactions of indi- viduals with LD may be less responsive (Mathinos, 1991) or appear less consistent, appropriate or flexible (Speckman, 1981). Such behav- ioural dispositions could in turn account for others' appraisal of the individual and subsequent responses.

Difficulties for many children with LD seem to arise from commu- nication problems resulting from a lack of linguistic sophistication (Donahue and Bryan, 1983). Thus, though the expressive language of individuals with LD may be similar to that of non-LD peers in mechan- ics and range of utterances, there tend to be problems in articulation of speech that affects the quality of social interactions. There are indica- tions that impaired communication skills of children with LD, both in linguistic and perceptual realms, results in the tone of their behaviour being different from that typical of others. Such behaviour may be different in subtle ways but viewed by peers as indicating children with LD to be cognitively less competent and thus less desirable as friends.

The social cognitive demands of given situations may also influence the behavioural responses of children with LD. Situations with ambiguous social cues tend to be more cognitively demanding for children with LD and therefore likely to elicit inappropriate behaviour (Gomez and Hazeldine, 1996; Pearl *et al.*, 1986). These difficulties illustrate the relationship between social cognition and behaviour. They also could explain problems experienced by children with LD in social relations as evidenced by the low regard with which they are held.

However, although the quality of social relations may be associated with behavioural dispositions, negative social experiences and patterns of behaviour associated with them seem different between children with LD and non-LD children. In sociometric terms, both children who are rejected and those who are neglected have few or no close friends. While some studies have reported a blurred distinction between these two categories (Musun-Miller, 1990), there are indications that children with fewer or no close friends (with few or no 'like most' nominations) tend to be rejected if they have LD, and neglected if they are non-LD children (Nabuzoka and Smith, 1993). Both these categories refer to children who are unpopular. However, rejected children receive more 'like least' or 'dislike' nominations and very few or no 'like most' nominations, whereas neglected children are characterized by low levels of both 'like most' and 'like least' nominations. Thus, unpopular children with LD (who tend to be rejected) are largely disliked, while most peers ignore unpopular non-LD children (who tend to be neglected).

In terms of associated behavioural attributes, both observational studies (Roberts *et al.*, 1991) and sociometric assessments (Nabuzoka and Smith, 1993) show no significant differences between children with LD and non-LD peers on negative behaviours that are disruptive or aggressive. These behaviours are associated with being liked least, and are therefore indicators of negative status for all children. As such, differences in social status of children with LD and those without cannot be accounted for solely by considerations of such children being aggressive and disruptive. It would appear, however, that behaviour associated with social adjustment of children with LD may be that which more uniquely reflects characteristics of learning disability.

For example, Nabuzoka and Smith (1993) found that children with LD were to a larger extent nominated on dimensions which reflected vulnerability or inadequacy (i.e. 'shy', 'seeks help', and 'victim of bullying') while non-LD children scored higher as peers who 'co-operate' and as 'leader'. Seeking help and being victims of bullying were associated with being liked least and may explain the peer rejection of children with LD. Being seen as co-operative was significantly associated with being liked most for all children. However, none of the children with LD met the criteria for classification as co-operative, and perhaps as a consequence none of them were in the popular status category.

Negative social status of some children with LD thus seems to be related to peer perceptions of being less co-operative, being victims of bullying and being seen as constantly in need of help. The attributes associated with each of these behavioural dispositions relate to competence in handling interpersonal situations. Being co-operative implies competence in interaction as it involves knowledge of social rules for turn-taking and reciprocity (Strain and Shores, 1977); being a victim of bullying implies vulnerability and a lack of competence in handling interpersonal conflict; and constantly seeking help implies a general lack of self-help as well as social skills. These attributes contribute to children with LD being perceived overall as cognitively less competent and thus less desirable. The behaviours of children with LD that are implicated in such perceptions would seem to be in situations that are cognitively too demanding for them. For example, children with LD require the constant support of teachers academically, but such attention can reinforce the negative view of constantly seeking help.

Summary and conclusions

While some problems of children with LD in peer relations are related to difficulties in understanding social situations, they cannot be explained solely by an absolute social cognitive deficit. Problems in the social cognitive domain can be context- or situation-specific, while developmental progression has also been observed. In addition, some behaviours that do not necessarily arise from social cognitive deficits could account for negative social relations.

Furthermore, while some behaviours may explain problems in social adjustment of all children, negative social experiences and the associated pattern of behaviours differ. For children with LD, therefore, the association of social cognition with adjustment may be through specific mediating behavioural attributes, which may be contingent on the specific cognitive demands of particular situations.

These observations have implications for interventions aimed at addressing the social problems faced by children with LD. Assessment of an individual child's level of functioning needs to account for variations in abilities across different contexts, and intervention strategies should be designed accordingly. The social cognitive model of functioning and adjustment offers some parameters for such assessment.

Chapter 7

Theoretical and methodological issues in research and intervention strategies

This chapter outlines a number of issues relevant to the study and understanding of the social development of children with learning disability (LD). First, theoretical and conceptual difficulties inherent in much of the work on characteristics and modes of functioning of children with LD are outlined and discussed. Methodological problems that make it difficult to judge the relevance and usefulness of research in this area are then specifically discussed.

Another concern is with issues related to applied research. Applied research is important in the development and refinement of effective strategies to meet the needs of children with LD. This involves evaluation of the impact of service design and provision, and of the design and efficacy of intervention approaches aimed at individual children. Integration or mainstreaming is an example of a service design with implications for social functioning and adjustment of children with LD. Specific issues of methodology and practical concerns in this area are therefore discussed at length. Regarding individualized intervention strategies, a number of these exist and have varying degrees of success. Some approaches aimed at enhancing social functioning are discussed to illustrate central concerns.

Discussion of each of these issues is accompanied by indications for future directions for research. Finally, some attention is devoted to discussing the necessity of integrating cognitive and social ecological research for a better understanding of the problems faced by children with LD in their social relations.

Theoretical issues

Debates have focused on whether children with LD are essentially developing differently in attaining developmental milestones in various domains, or simply developing more slowly. One alternative argument is to regard these perspectives as not necessarily mutually exclusive but to consider how developmental delays may reflect the different ways in which children with LD function (Dockrell and McShane, 1993). According to maturation theory, there is a sequential progression in the maturation of cognitive skills, and a child's ability in a specific cognitive area will depend on his or her maturational status (Piaget, 1970). Children with LD have been described as having a maturation lag reflecting slowness in certain aspects of neurological development, so they are seen as not being qualitatively different from normally developing peers, but rather just developing more slowly (Bender, 1957; Koppitz, 1973). In the domain of social development, some descriptions of children with LD have identified difficulties related to delays in social perception (Holder and Kirkpatrick, 1991; Nabuzoka and Smith, 1995) and social information processing (Nabuzoka, 1993) as characteristic of these children. These characteristics have then been associated with social problems (Spafford and Grosser, 1993; Kravetz *et al.*, 1999).

Differences between children with LD and non-LD peers in social cognitive functioning, and these being associated with other aspects of functioning such as behaviour, provides some evidence for what has been referred to as the *general interpersonal understanding mediation hypothesis*. According to this, the social difficulties of individuals with LD are mediated by the impairment of interpersonal understanding or other higher order cognitive processes (Kravetz *et al.*, 1999; Spafford and Grosser, 1993). Such cognitive difficulties might not necessarily reflect differences in the cognitive systems involved but perhaps in the ways they function. Kravetz *et al.* (1999) suggest a number of relations that should obtain if interpersonal understanding mediates the relationship between LD and difficulties in behavioural functioning. These are as follows:

- a positive relationship between LD and difficulties with social behaviour;
- a positive relationship between LD and impaired interpersonal understanding;
- a positive relationship between impaired interpersonal understanding and difficulties with social behaviour;
- a significant reduction in the relationship between LD and difficulties with social behaviour when impaired interpersonal understanding is controlled for.

In their study investigating aspects of these relationships, Kravetz and coworkers found firm confirmation for only the first three of the four (see Chapter 4). Regarding the fourth, they found that differences in classroom behaviour between children with LD and non-LD children remained statistically significant, though reduced, after controlling for interpersonal understanding. This suggested that the apparent misconduct of children with LD might only *partly* be due to their relative lack of interpersonal understanding. Other factors were also apparent-ly responsible for some of the differences. This differentiation in factors accounting for social difficulties of children with LD can perhaps best be understood if the etiological links between LD and these difficulties are considered to operate at two levels. These consist of a primary cause and a secondary cause of difficulties in social conduct.

According to the *primary cause hypothesis*, neurological impairments lead to learning problems such as comprehending written language. This same dysfunction is said to lead to problems in understanding non-verbal communication such as gestures and facial expressions (Spafford and Grosser, 1993). Such lack of social sensitivity could, in turn, undermine the social interactions of individuals with LD. The *secondary cause hypothesis*, too, attributes behavioural difficulties of children with LD to impairment in social cognition, while holding that the deficiencies evolve from a number of social experiences rather than neurological causes (Gresham and Elliot, 1989). Children with LD, for example, have fewer opportunities to engage in social interaction because they achieve less peer acceptance. This, in turn, may limit the accumulation of social experiences that would be the basis for inter-personal understanding. In other cases, the social difficulties of children with LD could emanate from such interpersonal processes as low self-esteem and feelings of inferiority in the face of academic and related difficulties.

On the whole, it is likely that both social cognitive processes and emotional and social consequences of LD may be implicated in the nature and quality of social relations experienced by children with LD – social adjustment. A revised model of social cognitive functioning and adjustment accounting for such social experiences and emotional adaptation is presented in Figure 7.1. In this model, the structure of interrelationships is such that social adjustment may also influence behavioural disposition in two ways. One way is that the nature of those peer relations may have implications for social–emotional adap-tation that may be reflected in manifest behaviours. For example, a child who is neglected by peers may become anxious about peer rela-tions and behave in an uncertain and shy manner. Such an outcome further limits the child's social contacts. Another path of influence involves the nature of the child's peer relations providing various levels of social experiences. As pointed out already, children excluded from peer interaction may lack those experiences that would be a basis for social understanding (social cognition).

Some of the evidence for the model depicted in Figure 7.1 has been provided in various studies reviewed in earlier chapters. Most of the evidence has been largely correlational. Though causative links can be inferred in the model, the complexity of the diagnosis of LD and the reciprocal nature of its consequences makes it difficult for a single field or correlational study to provide definite answers regarding eti-

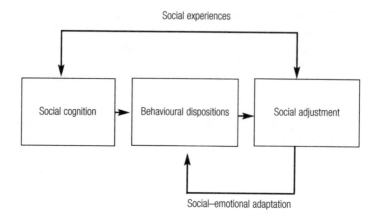

Figure 7.1 *A revised model of social cognitive functioning and adjustment accounting for social experiences and emotional adaptation*

ological links between variables related to social functioning and adjustment. In this respect, and for those concerned with preventive intervention, a social ecological approach to the psychological and social implications of LD may be more fruitful. Such an approach takes into account not only the children's functional levels, but also the different contexts in which problems associated with LD may occur. The school setting, though a single environment, provides various contexts for social relations. These contexts are best considered as providing relative risks for functional difficulties as well as opportunities for intervention. For example, the integrated setting provides some risks for the social emotional adjustment of children with LD while on the other hand it may be associated with improved social functioning of children with LD.

Methodological issues in conceptual and theoretical research

One major problem is that various studies have at times come up with different findings when carrying out similar investigations. Sometimes the findings directly contradict those from other studies. An example of this relates to the amount of positive behaviour by children with LD, compared with non-LD peers, in integrated settings. Some studies have found no differences between the two groups of children while others have found children with LD to be involved in more positive behaviour (Bryan *et al.*, 1976; Bryan, 1978). Another example of equivocal findings is the amount of time spent by children with LD interacting with teachers compared with non-LD peers (see Chapter 2). Some studies have reported children with LD to interact more with teachers (e.g. Roberts *et al.*, 1991; Siperstein and Goding, 1983), while others have reported less interaction (e.g. Mcintosh *et al.*, 1993).

A number of methodological problems possibly contribute to equivocal findings. For example, three factors have been identified as contributing to variable findings on positive behaviours. These include (a) characteristics of samples chosen for study, (b) functional domains assessed, and (c) the study measures used.

Sample characteristics

Variation across studies with regard to the nature and type of LD, age, gender, 'race' and culture, and peer status has at times confused and complicated the interpretation of research results, and precluded adequate cross-study comparisons.

Various studies have sought to address the possible confounding effects of sample characteristics by controlling for them. For example, some studies have focused solely on boys or girls, a specific age group, or even type of LD. These studies do provide information, but unfortunately it has only limited generalizability. In addition, while children do generally interact in groups in terms of gender, age and possibly 'race', intergroup interactions undoubtedly occur. The latter have implications for outcomes in functioning and adjustment of children with LD. For example, children with LD have been observed to interact more positively with younger but not same-age children (Bryan and Perlmutter, 1979).

The nature and type of LD
Some descriptions of characteristics associated with problems faced by children with LD have identified subtypes of disabilities. For example, Rourke (1989) posited two primary types: the non-verbal LD syndrome and the verbal (phonological) LD syndrome. Those with non-verbal LD are said to have poor overall social adaptation (due to social problem-solving deficits and difficulties identifying non-verbal communications) whereas those with verbal LD may not. The implications are that a lack of differentiation on this dimension is likely to lead to equivocal findings on measures of social adaptation. While some studies have sought to clarify the relative significance of verbal versus non-verbal LD on measures of social functioning, this distinction is not always made.

Age

The age of the subjects is another important factor. Research indicates that, although children with LD may not function at similar levels as non-LD peers of the same chronological age, effects of age differences amongst similarly diagnosed LD children can be expected (e.g. Gerber and Zinkgraf, 1982).

There are also some indications that the nature and severity of social problems may differ according to age. For example, it has been suggested that social–emotional development of students with LD may be more impaired in adolescence and early adulthood than previously thought (Huntington and Bender, 1993). Research has also shown that deficits in social competence of students with LD are observable across the age range (Calhoun and Beattie, 1987; Sater and French, 1989). However, some of these deficits may become more acute during the preadolescent years (Mellard and Hazel, 1992), corresponding with the increasing significance of the peer group.

While a number of studies have attempted to include a developmental dimension to their studies, there is still a need to incorporate this variable in many studies. In particular, there is a need for more longitudinal studies to document the developmental progression of functional and social emotional difficulties faced by individuals with LD. Such studies could follow individuals from the pre-school age through middle childhood and into adolescence or even early adulthood.

Gender

Gender effects have been observed on several variables, sometimes even interacting with age. Studies on perceptions of social cues such as emotions have generally shown few gender differences. However, an interaction of age and gender has been observed, with younger females with LD displaying difficulty interpreting emotions while older males may be inaccurate though rapid interpreters (Holder and Kirkpatrick, 1991).

Gender differences have also been observed on measures of social adjustment. Some studies on sociometric status, for example, have yielded findings indicating rejection to be particularly strong for girls with LD compared with boys with LD and non-LD girls (Kistner and Gatlin, 1989). There are also some suggestions that while children with LD tend to be victims of bullying significantly more than non-LD peers, girls with LD may particularly be at more risk than boys (Nabuzoka and Smith, 1993).

With regard to attitudes towards peers with LD, research indicates that girls tend to have more positive attitudes than boys (Rothlisberg *et al.*, 1994; Townsend *et al.*, 1993). However, boys may develop more positive attitudes on exposure to peers with LD while attitudes of girls may remain essentially unchanged (Nabuzoka and Rønning, 1997).

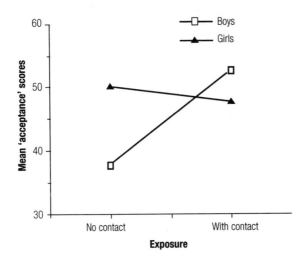

Figure 7.2 *Interaction of gender and exposure on acceptance of children with LD (Source: Nabuzoka and Rønning, 1997: 110)*

Such an interaction of gender with exposure on attitudes of non-LD children towards peers with LD is depicted in Figure 7.2.

These gender effects suggest that the social experiences of children with LD may vary between girls and boys. Gender differences in social functioning and adjustment have been recognized in many studies on children with LD. However, there appears to have been little effort in pursuing such differences as a specific line of inquiry. The tendency in most studies has been to focus solely on either boys or girls. Research is required, therefore, to focus more extensively on revealing the extent to which, and the manner in which, gender and LD status interact. Such research would more usefully inform the design of intervention strategies.

'Race' and culture

The racial characteristics of subjects is a variable that has received little attention in studies on social functioning and adjustment. A number of studies have documented the disproportionate representation of ethnic minority children in LD classes, or as having conduct problems (Peagam, 1994). There are also some indications that 'race' or ethnic minority status may be associated with the quality of interactions with others as reflected in some problems in peer relations (Kistner *et al.*, 1993; Schwarzwald and Hoffman, 1993).

Gresham and Reschly (1987b) examined sociometric differences between mainstreamed (integrated) students with mild LD and non-

LD black and white students. The results showed differential patterns of acceptance between black and white students with LD. White non-LD students had higher acceptance scores than black non-LD students, but black students with LD had higher acceptance scores than white students with LD. Gresham and Reschly suggested that the sample of white students with LD may have been more discrepant in terms of intellectual and academic performance than the black sample related to same-race non-LD peers, and thus perceived more negatively. Another explanation was that there might be racial and cultural differences in how children react to mild LD in educational settings.

What is clear from such findings, however, is that 'race' or ethnic status may interact with LD in measures of social functioning and adjustment. Details of 'race' or ethnic composition in samples as a specific variable to be examined are therefore important, especially for studies conducted in multi-ethnic contexts.

Another factor, related to gender and 'race', is the culture of the target children. Both gender and 'race' can interact with culture to influence the social functioning and adjustment of individual children, as they both involve socialization. On the one hand, general cross-study comparisons regarding the relationship between social functioning and adjustment of children with LD from different cultures can provide useful information about the generalizability of the relationships between social domains. For example, the data from Zambia regarding effects of various intervention approaches on the social functioning and adjustment of children with LD indicates the cross-cultural applicability of some intervention strategies (Rønning and Nabuzoka, 1993), and the effects of contact on attitudes towards children with LD (Favazza and Odom, 1997; Nabuzoka and Rønning, 1997). Such effects apparently apply to the various cultures studied. However, this may not necessarily mean that the specific modes of functioning and adjustment are comparable across the different cultures.

An example of specific cultural variation is social perception. Studies have generally indicated that children from different cultures can differentiate basic expressions of emotions by the age of 3 years and that this ability increases with age (Borke, 1973; Markham and Wang, 1996). However, there have also been cultural differences in the degree to which children of similar age may understand emotions (Joshi and MacLean, 1994; Markham and Wang, 1996). These differences have been attributed to different socialization practices, so that children are likely to perform better on emotion recognition in cultures where emphasis is put on the development of such skills. Thus, it is likely that a child with LD and a certain level of social perceptual skills (e.g. recognition of emotions) may have greater problems functioning in one culture requiring a high level of such skills and not in another. Similarly, while a child's apparently shy behaviour may be associated with adjustment problems in western culture, it may not necessarily be problematic in non-western societies, especially with regard to interactions with adults (Harkness and Super, 1982).

The point is that the definition of functional limitations in the social domain is likely to be culture-specific. In multicultural contexts and for children with LD, cultural variations may confound the social adjustment problems faced. For researchers, failure to recognize cultural variability across samples can make comparisons of findings difficult.

Peer status

Finally, peer status of the children studied is another possible reason for equivocal findings. In many studies the peer status of children with LD may not be formally assessed as a sample characteristic.

While children with LD may generally experience peer-related difficulties more than non-LD children, not all children with LD have problematic social relationships. Some research has indicated, for example, that there is a subgroup of adolescents with LD who are not rejected socially, but are rated as very similar to students without disabilities (Sabornie, 1990). It is likely that the children with LD who do not have problems in social relations also interact more positively with peers. Inconsistencies across various studies as to the social conduct of children with LD in general could thus also be attributable to the varying status of LD children. In this respect, studies reporting on measures of social functioning of children with LD should indicate whether the samples included children who had problems in peer relations.

Distinguishing domains and variables examined

There has sometimes been a lack of conceptual clarity about specific aspects and areas of the domains examined in various studies. This problem is manifested in attempts to identify the relationships between various domains and the variables that constitute them.

For example, there seems to be little consensus about the relationship between social competence and social adjustment. In some studies these concepts are treated synonymously while in others they are considered to represent separate, though related, aspects of social development. Another example of conceptual difficulty has been in attempts to distinguish social skills from social competence. One view that has been generally accepted is the suggestion by McFall (1982) of a distinction between social competence and social skill as trait and behaviour respectively (see also Gresham, 1986). According to McFall, social competence represents an evaluation based on judgements about whether or not a social task has been performed in a competent way. Social skills, on the other hand, are actions that may be exhibited in specific social situations and that require competent performance.

In this book, social adjustment is treated as, in part, an outcome of the interaction of variables related to social competence and social ecological factors. In this sense social competence refers to an evaluation of an individual's abilities such as social perception, social cognition and behaviour. These abilities constitute an individual's social skills and are reflected in outcomes for the individual and contribute to the social adjustment of that individual. Social adjustment, in turn, is partly an outcome of the individual's social competence, but also of social ecological factors such as how accommodating and accepting one's social setting is. For example, an individual from an ethnic minority background may not be well adjusted in a highly racist environment even though he or she is socially competent.

In the case of children with LD and as used in this context, social adjustment includes such variables as sociometric status and social acceptance, as well as the social–emotional well-being of the child, including satisfaction with social relations. Such a conceptualization permits a clear delineation of variables that may be associated with the quality of social relations experienced by children with LD. It also affords identification of specific areas in which children with LD may or may not be experiencing difficulties, thus enabling accurate targeting of intervention efforts.

Measuring and recording

One major methodological concern of all studies is the question of how to measure and record the phenomena under study. Operationalizing this does not appear to be a major problem in many studies on children with LD. The validity of these measures can, however, be questionable. For example, assessment of social functioning and adjustment often include behavioural measures and some index of social acceptance or sociometric status respectively. Behavioural measures, as an index of social functioning, are often obtained though a variety of methods. These include peer ratings or nominations, teacher ratings and direct observations. Both the behaviours selected for comparing the children and the methods used need to be sufficiently sensitive to detect meaningful differences between children with LD and non-LD children. For example, and as indicated in Chapter 5, teacher ratings and peer assessments may reflect different perceptions and sensitivity to various forms of behaviour by these assessors. In addition, the contexts and opportunities for observing target behaviours usually vary between assessors. The task, therefore, is to ensure that one is accurately measuring the most relevant behaviours for the domains being assessed.

Social acceptance or sociometric status, as a measure of the social adjustment of children, are often assessed by peer rating and peer nomination methods respectively. These are used to quantify the degree to which a child is liked or disliked by peers. However, peer ratings and peer nominations have been used to measure social functioning in some studies, and social adjustment in others. This may reflect a lack of conceptual differentiation between social functioning and adjustment. Another reason may, however, be more practical. For example, because peer nominations can be used for assessments of both behaviour and sociometric status, it is a convenient method for comparing the relationship between behavioural characteristics and sociometric status (as, for example, in Nabuzoka and Smith, 1993).

The peer nomination method such as that described by Coie *et al.* (1982) has been useful for a number of reasons (see Terry and Coie, 1991). First, extensive research has indicated the stability of status and predictability of negative outcomes for children identified as falling in various categories through this method (Coie and Dodge, 1983; Coie and Kupersmidt, 1983). Second, it facilitates examination of behavioural correlates of status groups and so can indicate profiles characteristic of children with LD. Third, despite some concerns about the use of negative nomination procedures, especially with regard to possible effects on children's subsequent behaviour, there has so far been no evidence to substantiate such concerns (Hayvren and Hymel, 1984). Alternative procedures that have been developed make assumptions about the number of nominations that are often difficult to meet (e.g. Newcomb and Bukowski, 1983), or are less accurate in identifying certain status groups such as neglected children (Asher and Dodge, 1986), or have poor long-term stability (Ollendick *et al.*, 1991).

Questions arise, however, as to the extent to which measures obtained through assessments by others – such as in peer nomination methods – actually reflect a child's overall social functioning or adjustment. This is important particularly where intervention is to be designed based on these measures. For example, some researchers have questioned the validity of using sociometric measurements without qualification. It is argued that such measures may not accurately reflect the social experiences of individual children as they rely too much on reports by others. A study by Ashley (1992), for example, indicates that certain discrepancies exist between the relationships described by the children and what actually happens in practice, especially with less well-adjusted children.

Ashley's study sought to examine the relationship between disruptive behaviour in the classroom and social adjustment as indicated by sociometric status and observations of peer group relationships. Boys aged 8–11 years were classified into three sets. One set comprised children retrospectively reported as disruptive by the infant department; another set consisted of highest-scoring children on sociometric measures; and a third set comprised the lowest-scoring children who were not disruptive. Sociometric measures were obtained for each child based on peer nominations, and the children were then ranked in order of sociometric status. The children were then observed in the playground over two terms. In addition Ashley had the children interviewed, during which they were asked who they most liked to play with, and why.

Ashley's study found a positive correlation between sociometric rank and the total number of interactions in the playground. There was, however, no significant correlation between rank and range of contacts (that is, the number of different children each child was observed to interact with). This suggested that children who received higher sociometric ranking were involved *more frequently* in interactions, but the actual *number* of children with whom they interacted was not significantly different from that of children of lower status. Thus, a child low in sociometric status ('isolate') was likely to interact with a range of as many different children as a 'sociometric star', but would be involved less frequently in this range of interactions. In this sense no child was actually isolated in the playground as implied by the sociometric category of 'isolate' (low-scoring on sociometric screening).

What emerged as a crucial factor was what Ashley called the 'reality of friendship' as indicated by mutuality of sociometric choice. Where friendship choices were mutual, it was likely that those relationships would be confirmed in practice. The high-status children had more mutual choices than either low-status groups (disruptive and non-disruptive), and these choices were associated with a general popularity factor. In this sense sociometry alone would be a useful measure of peer relations only for high-status children but not low-status children, particularly those who have problems in social relations. As children with LD tend to fall into the latter category, a more useful measure of social adjustment would be that which reflects actual patterns of social interaction experienced by the children.

According to Ashley, mutual choices are usually confirmed by observation and are therefore more reliable measures than sociometry alone. But as children with LD may also have low numbers of mutual choices, sociometric information would need to be supplemented by some observation of actual interaction patterns. This is particularly important if the measures are to be used to guide the design of intervention efforts. For example, a child who is very low in social status but shows a wide range of contacts in the playground may require a different form of intervention from that of a similarly low-status child but with a smaller range of contacts. The former could be characterized by inappropriate behaviours while the latter may be more withdrawn. While these two categories of children could be distinguished by the sociometric measures of being 'rejected' and 'neglected', one might benefit from intervention aimed at behavioural modification while the other might need training in social initiation skills. Clearly, multiple measures are required if a clear picture of the social adjustment of children with LD is to be obtained.

Applied research and intervention strategies

As with theoretical and conceptual research, applied research on children with LD raises a number of methodological issues. These relate to problems inherent in evaluating the efficacy of various forms of service provision and intervention approaches, such as integrating children with LD into mainstream schools. To demonstrate the success of programmes, one needs to show that children with LD have acquired the necessary skills and/or changes in behaviour. Service provision and intervention strategies can be evaluated in terms of social functioning and adjustment of the target children. There is, however, a difficulty in reaching firm conclusions about whether what is observed are effects of intervention or service provision.

Evaluating the type of provision and its impact

Applied research on service provision for children with LD mostly involves demonstrating the effects of integrated provision. A number of methodological problems have been identified with research in this area. Farrell (1997) points to some of the main issues raised in the literature:

- a lack of control groups in designs;
- the range of difficulties faced by children with LD;
- the variety of provision and/or treatment; and
- the interests of researchers.

Control groups
Research designs require control groups if 'treatment effects' are to be demonstrated. To demonstrate the effectiveness of integrated provision for children with LD, a matched group design should ideally be used. One group of children is placed in integrated provision and another 'matched' group is placed in a special school. A child in one group would be matched with another child in the other group on attributes likely to affect outcomes, such as age, gender, level of LD status, etc. Differences between the two groups can then be attributable to the type of provision experienced by the children (that is, whether integrated or in a special school).

However, such matched control group designs are virtually impossible, as there are ethical issues involved in allocating different provision to similar children solely for the purpose of research. In addition, it is difficult to match children with LD in such a way as to be certain that any two groups have the same relevant characteristics.

Range of difficulties

Difficulties faced by children vary so much that generalizing from one study to another is difficult. If one is to compare studies, it is necessary to be absolutely sure that they were conducted on similar children. This problem is compounded by the fact that studies from different countries may use varying terminology to refer to similar groups. Lewis (1995) points out, for example, that children designated as having 'severe learning difficulties' in the UK may be referred to as having 'moderate intellectual disabilities' in Australia and New Zealand, or 'moderate to severe mental retardation' in the US. Even then, Lewis points out, it is not clear whether such categories represent similar groups.

Variety of provision

It is not always easy to judge whether groups of children experienced similar or entirely different forms of integration. In the UK, different levels of integration exist both across and within education authorities. At the very minimum, a special unit may be placed in a mainstream school with children who have LD having 'opportunities' to interact with non-LD children at playtime or at lunchtime. Another type of integration involves children with LD attending some classes with their non-LD peers but being withdrawn to a 'resource' facility for other lessons. Sometimes terms such as 'functional integration' or 'social integration' have been used to distinguish situations where both groups of children take academic lessons together from situations where they come together only at playtime or lunchtime.

A third type of integration involves including children with disabilities in all mainstream activities, both academic and social, and this has been referred to as 'full integration'. In most cases this also requires a resource teacher or support worker being available to provide academic support to those with LD. This can have an effect on the success of integrating children with LD. It has been suggested, for example, that staff can facilitate the development of friendships between children with disabilities and mainstream peers by setting up conditions that encourage interactions (Hegarty, 1987). On the other hand, and as observed by Lynas (1986), the amount of attention paid to children with LD by staff can be a source of resentment for non-LD peers. The skills and sensitivity of the support staff as well as that of mainstream teachers are therefore other factors that research evaluating and comparing the efficacy of integrated settings needs to consider.

Objectivity

Evaluative research, especially when conducted and reported by those involved in the application of the service provision or intervention scheme, can suffer from a lack of objectivity. This is likely to be the case especially when the researchers have also been involved in the design of the scheme. It is then possible that the researchers might have a vested interest in showing that the scheme or type of service provision in question is effective. Thus, the only results that may be reported are those supportive of the preconceived views of the researchers. This problem is exacerbated by the reluctance of a significant number of journals to report 'negative' results.

Vested interests are difficult to verify. However, to eliminate suspicion of any such possibility, studies should report not only more detailed accounts of data gathering procedures and measures, but also any steps taken to avoid bias.

Effects of intervention strategies

Mere social ecological manipulations, such as placing children with LD amongst mainstream peers, do not automatically lead to positive outcomes. Research suggests that such efforts should be accompanied by an intervention strategy. The findings of studies reviewed in previous chapters have implications for the design of such intervention strategies. The social skill model of social adjustment, for example, suggests that intervention efforts should be directed at equipping children with skills that enhance their social competence. Thus, if problems faced by children with LD are associated with inappropriate behavioural dispositions (discussed in Chapter 5), intervention could appropriately be focused on changing the children's behaviours. Where the children are characterized by low levels of interaction patterns, efforts can be made to increase their ability to initiate interactions and to promote social responsiveness. Similarly, training in social perceptual and cognitive skills (Chapters 3 and 4) can enhance the social understanding of children with LD, leading to more appropriate behavioural responses and, subsequently, more positive social adjustment.

The role of social skills in interpersonal functioning was discussed in depth by Spence (1985), who also provided some guidelines for assessing and teaching these skills. The issues to be discussed in this section relate to problems in demonstrating the efficacy of these and a number of similar intervention approaches.

Various intervention strategies have been used to promote social interaction of children with disabilities into mainstream settings (Odom and Brown, 1993). These have included 'teacher-mediation' involving direct teacher (or support worker) modelling and reinforcement of social play (Fredricks *et al.*, 1978). In this approach the teacher or support worker interacts with children with LD in ways designed to increase positive behaviours with peers. However, there have been some indications that involvement of adults in this manner could impede child-to-child interactions (Lewis, 1995; Meyer *et al.*, 1987).

Another approach is 'peer-mediation', whereby normally developing (non-LD) children are trained to interact positively with children with LD. In studies where this approach has been used, levels of social interaction of children with LD have been observed to improve (Hundert and Houghton, 1992; Sainato *et al.*, 1992). In both these approaches, however, there have been some problems with maintenance over time and with generalization of the observed improvements across settings.

A more effective approach involving peer mediation places the focus mainly on the normally developing peers as agents of behaviour change (Odom and Brown, 1993; Odom and Strain, 1984; Strain and Odom, 1986). These peers would usually be trained in some operant techniques such as prompting and reinforcement, and are themselves prompted and reinforced for their performance with the children with disabilities. Despite the initial effects of peer-mediated approaches, however, these approaches have often shown limited generalization and maintenance effects across situations and time (Odom and Strain, 1984; Odom *et al.*, 1985). A review by Mathur and Rutherford (1991) identified subtypes of peer-mediated treatment. They concluded that these approaches demonstrate success in producing immediate, positive treatment effects, and that these effects may be generalizable. They point out, however, that systematic programming is required to produce lasting results.

Rønning and Nabuzoka (1993) suggested a number of explanations for the lack of maintenance of intervention effects. One was that studies have tended to be carried out within periods of time that were too short for any lasting relationships to develop between children. Children with LD spend too little time with their non-LD peers – during playtime – and may demonstrate a 'newcomer' pattern of shy, withdrawn behaviour. Another problem has been that the differentiation between peer- and teacher-mediated interventions can at times be unclear. Mathur and Rutherford (1991) pointed out, for example, that despite labelling of interventions as peer-mediated, teachers or support workers would still be in control in most cases. Rønning and Nabuzoka (1993) suggested that a more distinctive feature would be a situation where children with LD interacted with non-LD peers in the absence of adults.

Another reason for lack of maintenance of intervention effects could be the intensity of peer-mediated interventions. Most studies do not describe the intensity of the interventions, but one might assume that this is likely to be high bearing in mind the observed effects and relatively short times in which they are attained. It has also been suggested that there may be 'fatigue effects' causing the lack of maintenance (Odom and Strain, 1984). It has also been pointed out that applying interventions of high intensity within clearly defined time intervals or situations could also lead to the participants learning to discriminate between situations where target behaviours are to be performed and those where they should not. This would be contrary to the goal of obtaining generalized and durable interaction. It has been suggested that intervention studies should be conducted over much longer periods, and that long baselines should be applied initially to allow familiarization among the children.

The study by Rønning and Nabuzoka (1993) referred to in Chapter 5 addressed a number of issues related to the effects of interventions. Observations of the children's social interaction patterns were carried out in two situations: an 'experimental' situation where manipulations were made to investigate subsequent increases in social interaction, and a 'natural' situation without any manipulations. Several interventions, including social skills training, play skills training and prompting, and the 'special-friends' (peer-mediated) approaches, were tested at intervals separated by baselines. The findings showed some increases in interaction between children with LD and non-LD peers as a result of play skills training. However, training coupled with teacher prompts led to more substantial increases in interaction. The effects were transferred to the natural situation, but reduced in both situations when the intervention was withdrawn. The 'special friends' approach, associated with the non-LD children taking the role of initiators of interaction, led to increases in social behaviour in both the experimental and natural situations. These increases were maintained at both 1-month and 6-month follow-ups. In addition, and as indicated in Chapter 5, sociometric measures that were carried out during the course of the study showed increases in the status of children with LD. These increases in status were associated with the intervention programmes.

That study by Rønning and Nabuzoka demonstrates the differential effects of social skills training alone, social skills training with teacher prompts, and the use of non-LD peers as agents of social interactions ('special friends'). Each of these measures leads to improved positive social interaction by children with LD, which in turn seems to promote enhanced status among non-LD peers. Comparatively, teacher involvement in training and prompting of social interactions appears to lead to greater increases in such behaviour than does social skills training alone. There are indications that the gain resulting from such measures can be generalized to other situations, but there are some doubts about the lasting effects of applying teacher prompts as a way of promoting social interaction. The peer-mediated 'special friends' approach, on the other hand, seems effective in both increasing the social interaction of children with LD and non-LD peers and in the generalization and maintenance of such increases. In this approach, non-LD children act as trainers for children with LD, enabling them to become more efficient partners in play. They take on the role of initiating and prompting general play behaviours of children with LD, but do not engage in the training of specific elements of social skills such as basic verbal and non-verbal skills. It would appear that some incidental learning of such skills occurs as a consequence of these efforts. This point, however, needs to be verified by more focused research.

The acquisition of specific components of social skills (such as those related to social perception and social understanding), as a direct result of teacher- or peer-mediated approaches, can be inferred through patterns of behaviour that result from these interventions. Such skills may be demonstrated in the way children with LD become responsive to their social surroundings. One feature of increases in positive social interaction of children with LD, and resulting from peer-mediated approaches, has been that initiations for such interaction tend to be from non-LD peers. The gains for children with LD, from a functional point of view, are that they exhibit some increased capacity to respond appropriately and thereby sustain interaction with peers. This latter aspect not only suggests improved responsiveness, but also reflects greater social understanding. As for taking the initiative, a number of studies have indicated that training children with disabilities to initiate interaction does not often lead to generalized or durable changes (e.g. James and Egel, 1986). As discussed earlier, behavioural skills developed solely through intensified efforts of teachers or support workers often have problems of maintenance. However, peer-mediated approaches can also suffer from a failure to encourage children with LD to initiate social interaction.

Peer-mediated intervention is most effective where these agents or 'special friends' themselves are of high status and the main aim is to promote integration of children with LD into mainstream peer group activities. Then, even those non-LD children not designated any such responsibility take the initiative and instigate positive contacts with peers with LD (Sasso and Rude, 1987). Such a scenario, however, ascribes a dominant role to the non-LD children, which may inhibit social initiations by children with LD. This may particularly be the case with children with LD who are shy and withdrawn. Research generally suggests that even in those settings where integration has some apparent measure of success, the quality of discourse tends to be one-sided. Bayliss (1995), for example, found that communication between normally developing children and those with LD tended to be didactic whereby children with LD were often asked to respond to demands and not to interact on an equal basis.

The issue of concern is really whether children with LD can benefit from such interventions unless they are proactive. What may appear to be a general lack of initiative by children with LD may in fact reflect a lack of opportunity to exhibit acquired interactional skills. There is some evidence that children with LD can repeat linguistic skills learned from non-LD peers in appropriate contexts on different occasions, even where interaction in the mainstream context may have been didactic (Lewis, 1995). Such evidence has, however, largely been anecdotal and there are also some suggestions that effects of this nature may strongly depend on the cognitive levels of the children with LD (Howlin, 1994). More controlled research designs are needed.

Summary and conclusions

This chapter has outlined a number of issues relevant to the study and understanding of the social development of children with learning disabilities. Some of these relate to theoretical and conceptual difficulties inherent in much of the work on characteristics and modes of functioning of children with LD. A number of methodological problems make it difficult to judge the relevance and usefulness of much of the research that has been done. Three factors contributing to equivocal findings have been discussed: characteristics of the samples chosen for study, the functional domains assessed, and the study measures used. Some methodological problems are specifically related to applied research. Problems that arise relate to evaluation of the impact of service design and provision, and of the design and efficacy of intervention approaches aimed at individual children. Integration (or 'mainstreaming') is an example of a service design whose impact may not be easy to assess.

A number of individualized intervention strategies have been tried, with varying degrees of success. Some include training specific social skills in the areas in which children with LD have deficits. Others involve some training combined with increased opportunities for social interaction, including teacher-mediated and peer-mediated approaches. Both of these approaches have been shown to produce initial positive effects, but results have been equivocal on generalization and maintenance over time. Some evidence indicates that peer-mediated approaches are more promising if conducted in the context of natural peer group activities and over longer periods than just a few weeks.

Finally, a number of issues discussed in this book demonstrate the necessity of integrating social cognitive and social ecological research for a better understanding of the social problems faced by children with LD. For example, it is clear that the social setting can have a direct bearing on the functional levels of children with LD in a number of domains. Thus, gains in positive social behaviours have been observed in integrated school settings when compared with segregated ones. Such settings may, however, also have some implications for the social–emotional well-being of children with LD that may in turn affect their social cognitive functioning, and ultimately their behaviour. Unravelling the interactions between these variables and the domains they represent is a task for researchers. A number of efforts have already been put in place, and this book is one attempt at making sense of what is currently known.

References

Acton, N. (1982) The world's response to disability: evolution of a philosophy. *Archives of Physical Medicine and Rehabilitation*, 2, 145–149

Archie, V. W. and Sherrill, C. (1989) Attitudes toward handicapped peers of mainstreamed and nonmainstreamed children in physical education. *Perceptual and Motor Skills*, 69, 319–322

Asher, S. R. and Dodge, K. A. (1986) Identifying children who are rejected by their peers. *Developmental Psychology*, 22, 444–449

Asher, S. R. and Parker, J. G. (1989) Significance of peer relationship problems in childhood. In B. H. Scheider, G. Attili, J. Nadel and R. P. Weissberg (eds), *Social Competence in Developmental Perspective* (pp. 5–23), Dordrecht: Kluwer

Ashley, M. (1992) The validity of sociometric status. *Education Research*, 34(2), 149–154

Axelrod, L. (1982) Social perception in learning disabled adolescents. *Journal of Learning Disabilities*, 15, 610–613

Bachara, G. H. (1976) Empathy in learning disabled children. *Perceptual and Motor Skills*, 43, 541–542

Banerji, M. and Dailey, R. A. (1995) A study of the effects of an inclusion model on students with specific learning disabilities. *Journal of Learning Disabilities*, 28(8), 511–522

Baron, R. M. and Kenny, D. A. (1986) The moderator–mediator variable distinction in social psychological research: conceptual, strategic, and statistical consideration. *Journal of Personality and Social Psychology*, 51, 1173–1182

Baron-Cohen, S., Leslie, A. M. and Frith, U. (1985) Does the autistic child have a theory of mind? *Cognition*, 21, 37–46

Bayliss, P. (1995) Integration and interpersonal relations: interactions between disabled children and their non-disabled peers. *British Journal of Special Education*, 22(3), 131–140

Bender, L. (1957) Specific reading disability as maturation lag. *Bulletin of the Orton Society*, 7, 9–18

Bender, W. N. and Smith, J. K. (1990) Classroom behaviour of children and adolescents with learning disabilities: a meta-analysis. *Journal of Learning Disabilities*, 23, 298–305

Bickett, L. and Milich, R. (1990) First impressions formed of boys with learning disabilities and attention deficit disorder. *Journal of Learning Disabilities, 23*, 253–259

Borke, H. (1971) Interpersonal perception of young children: egocentrism or empathy? *Developmental Psychology, 5*, 263–269

Borke, H. (1973) The development of empathy in Chinese and American children between three and six years of age: a cross-cultural study. *Developmental Psychology, 9*, 102–108

Boulton, M. J. and Smith, P. K. (1994) Bully/victim problems in middle school children: stability, self perceived competence, peer perceptions, and peer acceptance. *British Journal of Developmental Psychology, 12*, 315–329

Boulton, M. J. and Underwood, K. (1992) Bully/victim problems among middle-school children. *British Journal of Educational Psychology, 62*, 73–87

Boyatzis, C. J. and Satyaprasad, C. (1994) Children's facial and gestural decoding and encoding: relations between skills and with popularity. *Journal of Nonverbal Behaviour, 18*(1), 37–55

Bretherton, I., Fritz, J., Zahn-Waxler, C. and Ridgeway, D. (1986) Learning to talk about emotions: a functionalist perspective. *Child Development, 57*, 529–548

Brody, L. (1985) Gender differences in emotional development: a review of theories and research. *Journal of Personality, 53*, 102–149

Bronfenbrenner, U. (1979) *The Ecology of Human Development: Experiments by Nature and Design*, Cambridge, MA: Havard University Press

Bruininks, V. L. (1978) Actual and perceived peer status of learning disabled students in mainstream programs. *Journal of Special Education, 12*, 51–58

Bruno, R. M. (1981) Interpretation of pictorially presented situations by learning disabled and normal children. *Journal of Learning Disabilities, 14*, 350–352

Bryan, J. H. and Perlmutter, B. (1979) Immediate impressions of LD children by female adults. *Learning Disability Quarterly, 2*, 80–88

Bryan, T. H. (1974a) An observational analysis of classroom behaviors of children with learning disabilities. *Journal of Learning Disabilities, 7*, 26–34

Bryan, T. H. (1974b) Peer popularity of learning disabled children. *Journal of Learning Disabilities, 7*, 621–625

Bryan, T. H. (1976) Peer popularity of learning disabled children: a replication. *Journal of Learning Disabilities, 9*, 307–311

Bryan, T. H. (1977) Learning disabled children's comprehension of non-verbal communication. *Journal of Learning Disabilities, 10*, 501–506

Bryan, T. H. (1978) Social relationships and verbal interactions of learning disabled children. *Journal of Learning Disabilities, 11*, 107–115

Bryan, T. H. & Bryan, J. H. (1978) *Understanding Learning Disabilities*, 2nd edn, Sherman Oaks, CA: Alfred

Bryan, T. H. and Bryan, J. H. (1981) Some personal and social experiences of learning disabled children. In B. K. Keogh (ed.), *Advances in Special Education: Vol.3* (pp. 147–186), Greenwich, CT: JAI Press

Bryan, T. H., Donahue, M. and Pearl, R. (1981a) Learning disabled children's peer interactions during a small-group problem solving task. *Learning Disability Quarterly, 4*, 13–22

Bryan, T. H., Donahue, M., Pearl, R. and Sturm, C. (1981b) Learning disabled children's conversational skills: the 'TV Talk Show'. *Learning Disability Quarterly*, 4, 260–270

Bryan, T. H., Werner, M. and Pearl, R. (1982) Learning disabled students' conformity responses to prosocial and antisocial situations. *Learning Disability Quarterly*, 5, 344–352

Bryan, T. H., Wheeler, R., Felcan, J. and Henek, T. (1976) 'Come on, Dummy': an observational study of children's communications. *Journal of Learning Disabilities*, 9, 53–61

Bullock, M. and Russell, J. A. (1986) Conceptual emotions in developmental psychology. In C. E. Izard and P. Read (eds), *Measurement of Emotions in Children: Vol. 2* (pp. 203–237), New York: Cambridge University Press

Butler, R. and Marinov-Glassman, D. (1994) The effects of educational placement and grade level on the self-perceptions of low achievers and students with learning disabilities. *Journal of Learning Disabilities*, 27(5), 325–334

Buysse, V. and Bailey, D. B. (1993) Behavioral and developmental outcomes in young children with disabilities in integrated and segregated settings: a review of comparative studies. *Journal of Special Education*, 26, 434–461

Calhoun, M. L. and Beattie, J. (1987) Social competence needs of mildly handicapped adolescents. *Adolescence*, 22, 555–563

Campos, J. J., Barrett, K. C., Lamb, M. E., Goldsmith, H. H. and Sternberg, C. (1983) Socioemotional development. In M. M. Haith and J. J. Campos (eds), *Handbook of Child Psychology: Vol. 2. Infancy and Developmental Psychobiology* (pp. 783–915), New York: John Wiley

Camras, L. A. (1986) Judgement of emotion from facial expression and situational context. In C. E. Izard and P. Read (eds), *Measuring Emotions in Infants and Children, Vol. 2* (pp. 75–79), Cambridge: Cambridge University Press

Cardell, C. D. and Parmar, R. S. (1988) Teacher perceptions of temperament characteristics of children classified as learning disabled. *Journal of Learning Disabilities*, 21, 497–502

Carlson, C. I. (1987) Social interaction goals and strategies of children with learning disabilities. *Journal of Learning Disabilities*, 20, 306–311

Cavallaro, S. A. and Porter, R. H. (1980) Peer preferences of at-risk and normally developing children in preschool mainstream classrooms. *American Journal of Mental Deficiency*, 84, 357–366

Chalmers, J. B. and Townsend, M. A. R. (1990) The effects of training in social perspective taking on socially maladjusted girls. *Child Development*, 61, 178–190

Chandler, M. J. (1977) Social cognition: a selective review of current research. In W. F. Overton and J. M. Gallagher (eds), *Knowledge and Development: Vol. 1. Advances in Research and Theory* (pp. 93–147), New York: Plenum

Chapman, J. W. and Boersma, F. J. (1979) Learning disabilities, locus of control and mother attitudes. *Journal of Educational Psychology*, 71, 250–258

Charlesworth, W. and Kreutzer, M. (1973) Facial expressions of infants and children. In P. Ekman (ed.), *Darwin and Facial Expression* (pp. 91–168) New York: Academic Press

Cillessen, A. H. N. (1991) *The Self-perpetuating Nature of Children's Peer Relationships*, doctoral dissertation, Catholic University of Nijmegen, The Netherlands

Clements, J. (1987) *Severe Learning Disability and Psychological Handicap*. Chichester: John Wiley

Coie, J. D. and Dodge, K. A (1983) Continuities and changes in children's social status: a five-year longitudinal study. *Merrill–Palmer Quarterly*, 29, 261–282

Coie, J. D. and Dodge, K. A. (1988) Multiple sources of data on social behaviour and social status in the school: a cross-age comparison. *Child Development*, 59, 815–829

Coie, J. D., Dodge, K. A. and Cappotelli, H. (1982) Dimensions and types of social status: a cross-age perspective. *Developmental Psychology*, 18, 557–570

Coie, J. D., Dodge, K. A. and Kupersmidt, J. B. (1990) Peer group behaviour and social status. In S. R. Asher and J. D. Coie (eds), *Peer Rejection in Childhood*, Cambridge: Cambridge University Press

Coie, J. D. & Kupersmidt, J. (1983) A behavioral analysis of emerging social status in boys' groups. *Child Development*, 54, 1400–1416

Coleman, J. M. (1983) Handicapped labels and instructional segregation: influences on children's self-concepts versus the perceptions of others. *Learning Disability Quarterly*, 6, 3–11

Cook, E. T., Greenberg, M. T. and Kusche, C. A. (1994) The relations between emotional understanding, intellectual functioning, and disruptive behavior problems in elementary school-aged children. *Journal of Abnormal Child Psychology*, 22(2), 205–219

Crick, N. R. and Dodge, K. A. (1994) A review and reformulation of social information processing mechanisms in children's social adjustment. *Psychological Bulletin*, 115, 74–101

Demchak, M. and Drinkwater, S. (1992) Preschoolers with severe disabilities: the case against segregation. *Topics in Early Childhood Special Education*, 11(4), 70–83

Denham, S. A. and Couchoud, E. A. (1990) Young preschoolers' understanding of emotions. *Child Study Journal*, 20(3), 171–191

Department for Education and Employment (DfEE) (2000) *Bullying: Don't Suffer in Silence – An Anti-bullying Pack for Schools*, London: HMSO

Department of Health & Social Security (DHSS) (1980) *Mental Handicap: Progress, Problems and Priorities* (a review of mental handicap services in England since the 1971 White paper, 'Better Services for the Mentally Handicapped'), London: HMSO

Dickstein, E. B. and Warren, D. R. (1980) Role-taking deficits in learning disabled children. *Journal of Learning Disabilities*, 13, 378–382

Dimitrovsky, L. (1964) The ability to identify the emotional meaning of vocal expressions at successive age levels. In J. R. Davitz (ed.), *The Communication of Emotional Meaning* (pp. 69–86), New York: McGraw-Hill

Dimitrovsky, L., Spector, H., Levy-Shiff, R. and Vakil, E. (1998) Interpretation of facial expressions of affect in children with learning disabilities with verbal or nonverbal deficits. *Journal of Learning Disabilities*, 31(3), 286–292 and 312

Dockrell, J. and McShane, J. (1993) *Children's learning difficulties: A cognitive approach*, Oxford: Blackwell

Dodge, K. A. (1983) Behavioral antecedents of peer social status. *Child Development*, 54, 1386–1399

Dodge, K. A. (1986) A social information processing model of social competence in children. In M. Perlmutter (ed.), *Cognitive Perspectives on Children's Social and Behavioural Development. The Minnesota Symposia on Child Psychology: Vol. 18* (pp. 77–125), Hillsdale, NJ: Lawrence Erlbaum

Dodge, K. A., Coie, J. D. and Brakke, N. P. (1982) Behaviour patterns of socially rejected and neglected preadolescents: the roles of social approach and aggression. *Journal of Abnormal Child Psychology*, 10, 389–410

Dodge, K. A. and Feldman, E. (1990) Issues in social cognition and sociometric status. In S. R. Asher and J. D. Coie (eds), *Peer Rejection in Childhood*, Cambridge: Cambridge University Press

Dodge, K. A. and Frame, C. L. (1982) Social cognitive biases and deficits in aggressive boys. *Child Development*, 53, 620–635

Dodge, K. A., Murphy, R. M. and Buchsbaum, K. (1984) The assessment of intention: – cue detection skills in children: implications for developmental psychopathology. *Child Development*, 55, 163–173

Dodge, K. A. and Newman, J. P. (1982) Biased decision making processes in aggressive boys. *Journal of Abnormal Psychology*, 90, 375–379

Dodge, K. A., Pettit, G. S., McClaskey, C. L. and Brown, M. M. (1986) Social competence in children. *Monographs of the Society for Research in Child Development*, 51 (2 Serial No. 213)

Donahue, M. and Bryan, T. (1983) Conversational skills and modeling in learning disabled boys. *Applied Psycholinguistics*, 4, 251–278

Edmondson, B., deJung, J., Leland, H. and Leach, E. (1974) *The Test of Social Inference*, New York: Educational Activities

Esposito, B. G. and Peach, W. J. (1983) Changing attitudes of preschool children toward handicapped persons. *Exceptional Children*, 49, 361–363

Farrell, P. (1997) The integration of children with severe learning difficulties: a review of the recent literature. *Journal of Applied Research in Intellectual Disabilities*, 10(1), 1–14

Favazza, P. C. and Odom, S. L. (1997) Promoting positive attitudes of kindergarten-age children toward people with disabilities. *Exceptional Children*, 63, 405–418

Feagans, L. and McKinney, J. D. (1981) The pattern of exceptionality across domains in learning disabled children. *Journal of Applied Developmental Psychology*, 1, 313–328

Fish, J. (1985) *Educational Opportunities for All?* London: Inner London Education Authority

Fisher, B. L, Allen, R. and Kose, G. (1996) The relationship between anxiety and problem-solving skills in children with and without learning disabilities. *Journal of Learning Disabilities*, 29, 439–446

Flicek, M. and Landau, S (1985) Social status problems of learning-disabled and hyperactive/learning-disabled boys. *Journal of Clinical Child Psychology*, 14, 340–344

Foster, S. L., DeLawyer, D. B. and Guevremont, D. C., (1985) Selecting targets for social skills training with children and adolescents. In K. D. Gadow (ed.), *Advances in Learning and Behavioral Disabilities: Vol. 4*, Greenwich, LT: JAI Press

Fredricks, H., Baldwin, V., Grove, D., Moore, W., Riggs, C. and Lyons, B. (1978) Integrating the moderately and severely handicapped preschool child into a normal day care setting. In M. Guralnick (ed.), *Early Intervention and the Integration of Handicapped and Nonhandicapped Children*, Baltimore: University Park Press

French, D. C. (1988) Heterogeneity of peer rejected boys: aggressive and nonaggressive subtypes. *Child Development*, 59, 976–985

Fryxell, D. and Kennedy, C. H. (1995) Placement along the continuum of services and its impact on students' social relationships. *Journal of the Association for Persons with Severe Handicaps*, 20, 259–269

Furman, W. (1984) Issues in the assessment of social skills of normal and handicapped children. In T. Field, J. L. Roopnarine and M. Segal (eds), *Friendships in Normal and Handicapped Children*, New Jersey: Ablex

Garber, J. (1984) Classification of childhood psychopathology: a developmental perspective. *Child Development*, 55, 30–48

Garrett, M. K. and Crump, W. D. (1980) Peer acceptance, teacher references, and self-appraisal of social status among learning disabled students. *Learning Disability Quarterly*, 3, 42–48

Gerber, M. M. (1983) Learning disabilities and cognitive strategies: a case for training or constraining problem solving? *Journal of Learning Disabilities*, 16, 255-259

Gerber, P. J. and Zinkgraf, S. A. (1982) A comparative study of social–perceptual ability in learning disabled and nonhandicapped students. *Learning Disability Quarterly*, 5, 374–378

Gitter, A., Mostofsky, D. and Quincy, A. (1971) Race and sex differences in the child's perception of emotion. *Child Development*, 42, 2071–2075

Gnepp, J. (1983) Children's social sensitivity: infering emotions from conflicting cues. *Developmental Psychology*, 19, 805–814

Gnepp, J. and Hess, D. L. R. (1986) Children's understanding of verbal and facial display rules. *Developmental Psychology*, 22, 103–108

Goethals, G. R. (1986) Social comparison theory: psychology from the lost and found. *Personality and Social Psychology Bulletin*, 12, 261–278

Goldfried, M. R. and d'Zurilla, T. J. (1969) A behavioural–analytic model for assessing competence. In C. D. Spielberger (ed.), *Current Topics in Clinical and Community Psychology: Vol. 1* (pp. 151–196), New York: Academic Press

Goldman, J. A. (1981) Social participation of preschool children in same- versus mixed-age groups. *Child Development*, 52, 644–650

Gomez, R. and Hazeldine, P. (1996) Social information processing in mildly mentally retarded children. *Research in Developmental Disabilities*, 17(3), 217–227

Gottlieb, J. (1981) Mainstreaming: fulfilling the promise? *American Journal of Mental Deficiency*, 86, 115–126

Gottlieb, J., Semmel, M. I. and Veldman, D. J. (1978) Correlates of social status among mainstreamed mentally retarded children. *Journal of Educational Psychology*, 70, 396–405

Gray, J. M., Fraser, W. L. and Leudar, I. (1983) Recognition of emotion from facial expression in mental handicap. *British Journal of Psychiatry*, 142, 566–571

Gresham, F. M. (1986) Conceptual issues in the assessment of social competence in children. In P. Strain, M. Guralnick and H. Walker (eds), *Children's Social Behaviour: Development, Assessment, and Modification* (pp. 143–179), Orlando, FL: Academic Press

Gresham, F. M. and Elliot, S. N. (1987) The relationship between adaptive behaviour and social skills: issues in definition and assessment. *Journal of Special Education*, 21, 167–181

Gresham, F. M. and Elliott, S. N. (1989) Social skills deficits as primary learning disability. *Journal of Learning Disabilities*, 22, 120–124

Gresham, J. M. and Reschly, D. J. (1986) Social skills deficits and low acceptance of mainstreamed learning disabled children. *Learning Disability Quarterly*, 9, 23–32

Gresham, F. and Reschly, D. J. (1987a) Dimensions of social competence: method factors in the assessment of adaptive behaviour, social skills, and peer acceptance. *Journal of School Psychology*, 25, 367–382

Gresham, F. M. and Reschly, D. J. (1987b) Sociometric differences between mildly handicapped black and white students. *Journal of Educational Psychology*, 79, 195–197

Grolnick, W. S. and Ryan, R. M. (1990) Self-perceptions, motivation and adjustment in children with learning disabilities: a multiple group comparison study. *Journal of Learning Disabilities*, 23, 177–184

Gross, A. L. and Ballif, B. (1991) Children's understanding of emotion from facial expressions and situations: a review. *Developmental Review*, 11, 368–398

Guralnick, M. J. (1976) The value of integrating handicapped and nonhandicapped preschool children. *American Journal of Orthopsychiatry*, 46, 236–245

Guralnick, M. J. (1978) Integrated preschools as educational and therapeutic environments: concepts, design, and analysis. In M. J. Guralnick (ed.), *Early Intervention and the Integration of Handicapped and Nonhandicapped Children* (pp. 115–145), Baltimore: University Park Press

Guralnick, M. J. (1981) The social behavior of preschool children at different developmental levels: effects of group composition. *Journal of Experimental Child Psychology*, 31, 115–130

Guralnick, M. J. (1986) The application of child development principles and research to preschool mainstreaming. In C. J. Meisel (ed.), *Mainstreaming Handicapped Children: Outcomes, Controversies, and New Directions* (pp. 21-41), Hillsdale, NJ: Lawrence Erlbaum

Guralnick, M. J. (1990) Major accomplishments and future directions in early childhood mainstreaming. *Topics in Early Childhood Special Education*, 10(2), 1–17

Guralnick, M. J. and Groom, J. M. (1988) Peer interactions in mainstreamed and specialised classrooms: a comparative analysis. *Exceptional Children*, 54, 415–425

Gurucharri, C. and Selman, R. L. (1982) The development of interpersonal understanding during childhood, preadolescence, and adolescence: a longitudinal follow-up study. *Child Development*, 53, 924–927

Haager, D. and Vaughn, S. (1995) Parent, teacher, peer, and self-reports of the social competence of students with learning disabilities. *Journal of Learning Disabilities*, 28(4), 205

Hall, J. (1978) Gender effects in decoding nonverbal cues. *Psychological Bulletin*, 85, 845–857

Hallahan, D. P. and Kauffman, J. M. (1976) *Introduction to Learning Disabilities: A Psychobehavioral Approach*, Englewoods Cliffs, NJ: Prentice-Hall

Hallahan, D. P. and Kauffman, J. M. (1977) Labels, categories, behaviors: ED, LD, and EMR reconsidered. *Journal of Special Education*, 11, 139–149

Harkness, S. and Super, C. M. (1982) Why African children are so hard to test. In L. L. Adler (ed.), *Cross-cultural Research at Issue* (pp. 145–152), New York: Academic Press

Harris, P. L. (1989) *Children and Emotion: The Development of Psychological Understanding*, Oxford: Blackwell

Harrist, A. W., Zaia, A. F., Bates, J. E., Dodge, K. A. and Pettit, G. S. (1997) Subtypes of social withdrawal in early childhood: sociometric status and socio-cognitive differences across four years. *Child Development*, 68, 278–294

Hartup, W. W. (1983) Peer relations. In E. M. Hetherington (ed.), *Handbook of Child Psychology: Vol. 4. Socialisation, Personality, and Social Development* 4th edn (pp. 103–196), New York: John Wiley

Hartup, W. W. (1989) Behavioural manifestations of children's friendships. In T. J. Berndt and G. W. Ladd (eds), *Peer Relationships in Child Development* (pp. 46–70), New York: John Wiley

Hayvren, M. and Hymel, S. (1984) Ethical issues in sociometric testing: the impact of sociometric measures on interactive behaviour. *Developmental Psychology*, 20, 844–849

Hegarty, S. (1987) *Meeting Special Needs in Ordinary Schools*, London: Cassell

Heinman, T. and Margalit, M. (1998) Loneliness, depression, and social skills among students with mild mental retardation in different educational settings. *Journal of Special Education*, 32(3), 154–163

Hiatt, S. W., Campos, J. J. and Emde, R. N. (1979) Facial patterning and infant emotional expression: happiness, surprise and fear. *Child Development*, 50, 1020–1035

Hobson, R. P. (1986a) The autistic child's appraisal of expressions of emotion. *Journal of Child Psychology and Psychiatry*, 27, 321–342

Hobson, R. P. (1986b) The autistic child's appraisal of expressions of emotion: a further study. *Journal of Child Psychology and Psychiatry*, 27, 671–680

Hoffman, M. L. (1977) Sex differences in emphathy and related behaviours. *Psychological Bulletin*, 84, 712–722

Hoffner, C. and Badzinski, D. M. (1989) Children's integration of facial and situational cues to emotion. *Child Development*, 60, 411–422

Holder, H. B. and Kirkpatrick, S. W. (1991) Interpretation of emotions from facial expressions in children with and without learning disabilities. *Journal of Learning Disabilities*, 24, 170–177

Horowitz, E. C. (1981) Popularity, decentering ability, and roletaking skills in learning disabled and normal children. *Learning Disability Quarterly*, 4, 23–30

Howlin, P. (1994) Special educational treatment. In M. Rutter, E. Taylor and L. Hersov (eds), *Child and Adolescent Psychiatry: Modern Approaches*, 3rd edn, Oxford: Blackwell

Hubbard, J. A. and Coie, J. D. (1994) Emotional correlates of social competence in children's peer relationships. *Merrill–Palmer Quarterly Journal of Developmental Psychology*, 40(1), 1–20

Hundert, J. and Houghton, A. (1992) Promoting social interaction of children with disabilities in integrated preschools: a failure to generalise. *Exceptional Children*, 58, 311–320

Huntington, D. D. and Bender, W. N. (1993) Adolescents with learning disabilities at risk? Emotional well-being, depression, suicide. *Journal of Learning Disabilities*, 26, 159–166

Hyman, H. H. and Singer, E. (1976) An introduction to reference group theory. In E. P. Hollander and R. G. Hunt (eds), *Current Perspectives in Social Psychology*, 2nd edn (pp. 87–97), New York: Oxford University Press

Hymel, S. and Rubin, K. H. (1985) Children with peer relationships and social skills problems: conceptual, methodological, and developmental issues. In G. J. Whitehurst (ed.), *Annals of Child Development: Vol. 2* (pp. 251–297), Greenwich, CT: JAI Press

Izard, C. E. (1971) *The Face of Emotion*, New York: Appleton–Century–Crofts

Jackson, S. C., Enright, R. D. and Murdock, J. Y. (1987) Social perception problems in adolescents with learning disabilities: developmental lags versus perceptual deficit. *Journal of Learning Disabilities*, 20, 361–364

James, S. D. and Egel, A. L. (1986) A direct prompting strategy for increasing reciprocal interactions between handicapped and nonhandicapped siblings. *Journal of Applied Behavior Analysis*, 19, 173–187

Janney, R. E., Snell, M. A., Beers, M. K. and Raynes, M. (1995) Integrating students with moderate and severe disabilities into general education classes. *Exceptional Children*, 61, 425–439

Jenkins, J. R. and Odom, S. L. and Speltz, M. L. (1989) Effects of social integration on preschool children with handicaps. *Exceptional Children*, 55, 420–428

Johnson, D. J and Myklebust, H. R. (1967) *Learning Disabilities: Educational Principles and Practices*. New York: Grune & Stratton

Jorm, A. F., Share, D. L., Matthews, R. and Maclean, R (1986) Behavior problems in specific reading-retarded and general reading-backward children: a longitudinal study. *Journal of Child Psychology and Psychiatry*, 27, 33–43

Joshi, M. S. and MacLean, M. (1994) Indian and English children's understanding of the distinction between real and apparent emotion. *Child Development*, 65, 1364–1376

Juvonen, J. and Bear, G. (1992) Social adjustment of children with and without learning disabilities in integrated classrooms. *Journal of Educational Psychology*, 84, 322–330

Kavale, K. A. and Forness, S. R. (1996) Social skill deficits and learning disabilities: a meta-analysis. *Journal of Learning Disabilities*, 29, 226–257

Kennedy, C. H., Shukla, S. and Fryxell, D. (1997) Comparing the effects of educational placement on the social relationships of intermediate school students with severe disabilities. *Exceptional Children*, 64, 31–47

Kirk, S. A. (1962) *Educating the Exceptional Children*, Boston: Houghton Miffin

Kirk, S. A. (1963) Behavioural diagnosis and remediation of learning disabilities. In *Proceedings of the Annual Conference on Exploration into the Problems of the Perceptually Handicapped Child* (pp. 1–7), Evanston, IL: Fund for Perceptually Handicapped Children

Kistner, J. A. and Gatlin, D. (1989a) Correlates of peer rejection among children with learning disabilities. *Learning Disability Quarterly*, 12, 133–140

Kistner, J. A. and Gatlin, D. F. (1989b) Sociometric differences between learning-disabled and nonhandicapped students: effects of sex and race. *Journal of Educational Psychology*, 81, 118–120

Kistner, J., Haskett, M., White, K. and Robbins, F. (1987) Perceived competence and self worth of LD and normally achieving students. *Learning Disability Quarterly*, 10, 37–44

Kistner, J., Metzler, A., Gatlin, D. and Risi, S. (1993) Classroom racial proportions and children's peer relations: race and gender effects. *Journal of Educational Psychology*, 85, 446–452

Kochenderfer, B. J. and Ladd, G. W. (1996) Peer victimization: cause or consequence of school maladjustment? *Child Development*, 67, 1305–1317

Koppitz, E. (1973) Special class pupils with learning disabilities: a five-year follow-up study. *Academic Therapy*, 8, 133–140

Kravetz, S., Faust, M., Lipshitz, S. and Shalhav, S. (1999) LD, interpersonal understanding, and social behaviour in the classroom. *Journal of Learning Disabilities*, 32, 248–255

Kurdek, L. A. and Krile, D. (1982) A developmental analysis of the relation between peer acceptance and both interpersonal understanding and perceived social competence. *Child Development*, 53, 1485–1491

Ladd, G. W. (1989) Toward a further understanding of peer relationship and their contribution to child development. In T. J. Berndt and G. W. Ladd (eds), *Peer Relationships in Child Development* (pp. 1–11), New York: John Wiley

LaGreca, A. M. (1981) Social behaviour and social perception in learning disabled children: a review with implications for social skills training. *Journal of Pediatric Psychology*, 6, 395–416

Lewis, A. (1995) *Children's Understanding of Disability*, London: Routledge

Little, S. S. (1993) Nonverbal learning disabilities and socioemotional functioning: a review of recent literature. *Journal of Learning Disabilities*, 26, 653–665

Lynas, W. (1986) Pupils' attitudes to integration. *British Journal of Special Education*, 13(1), 31–33

MacMillan, D. L., Gresham, F. M. and Bocian, K. M. (1998) Discrepancy between definitions of learning disabilities and school practices: an empirical investigation. *Journal of Learning Disabilities*, 31, 314–326

MacMillan, D. C. and Morrison, G. M. (1984) Sociometric research in special education. In R. L. Jones (ed.), *Attitudes and Attitude Change in Special Education: Theory and Practice* (pp. 93–117), Reston, VA: Council for Exceptional Children

Maheady, L. and Sainato, D. M. (1986) Learning-disabled students' perception of social events. In S. J. Ceci (ed.), *Handbook of Cognitive, Social, and Neuropsychological Aspects of Learning Disabilities: Vol. 1*, Hillsdale, NJ: Lawrence Erlbaum

Margalit, M. (1998) Loneliness and coherence among preschool children with learning disabilities. *Journal of Learning Disabilities*, 31(2), 173–180

Margalit, M. and Efrati, M. (1996) Loneliness, coherence and companionship among children with learning disorders. *Educational Psychology*, 16, 69–79

Markham, R. and Wang, L. (1996) Recognition of emotion by Chinese and Australian children. *Journal of Cross-Cultural Psychology*, 27, 616–643

Martlew, M. and Cooksey, C. (1989) The integration of a child with cerebral palsy into a mainstream nursery. *European Journal of Special Educational Needs*, 4, 103–116

Martlew, M. and Hodson, J. (1991) Children with mild learning difficulties in an integrated and in a special school: comparisons of behaviour, teasing and teachers' attitudes. *British Journal of Educational Psychology*, 61, 355–372

Mathinos, D. A. (1991) Conversational engagement of children with learning disabilities. *Journal of Learning Disabilities*, 24, 439–446

Mathur, S. R. and Rutherford, R. B. (1991) Peer-mediated interventions promoting social skills of children and youth with behavioural disorders. *Education and Treatment of Children*, 14, 227–242

McConaughy, S. H. and Ritter, D. R. (1986) Social competence and behavioural problems of learning disabled boys aged 6–11. *Journal of Learning Disabilities*, 19, 39–45

McFall, R. M. (1982) A review and reformulation of the concept of social skills. *Behavioural Assessment*, 4, 1–33

McHugh, P. (1970) A common-sense conception of deviance. In J. D. Douglas (ed.), *Deviance and Respectability: The Social Construction of Moral Meanings* (pp. 61–88), New York: Basic Books

Mcintosh, R., Vaughn, S., Schumm, J. S., Haager, D. and Lee, O. (1993) Observations of students with learning disabilities in general education classrooms. *Exceptional Children*, 60, 249–261

McLoughlin, J. A., Clark, F. L., Mauck, A. R. and Petrosko, J. (1987) A comparison of parent–child perceptions of student learning disabilities. *Journal of Learning Disabilities*, 20, 357–368

McMichael, P. (1980) Reading difficulties, behavior and social status. *Journal of Educational Psychology*, 72, 76–86

McQuitty, L. L. (1957) Elementary linkage analysis for isolating orthogonal and oblique types and typal relevancies. *Educational and Psychological Measurement*, 17, 207–229

Mellard, D. F. and Hazel, J. S. (1992) Social competencies as a pathway to successful life transitions. *Learning Disability Quarterly*, 15, 251–271

Merrell, K. W. (1991) Teacher ratings of social competence and behavioural adjustment: differences between learning-disabled, low-achieving, and typical students. *Journal of School Psychology*, 29, 207–217

Meyer, L. H., Fox, A., Schermer, A., Ketelsen, D., Montan, N., Maley, K. and Cole, D. (1987) The effects of teacher intrusion on social play interactions between children with autism and their nonhandicapped peers. *Journal of Autism and Developmental Disorders*, 17, 315–332

Mills, P. E., Cole, K. N., Jenkins, J. R. and Dale, P. S. (1998) Effects of differing levels of inclusion on preschoolers with disabilities. *Exceptional Children*, 65, 79–90.

Morris, L., Watt, J. and Wheatley, P. (1995) Pupils with special needs: A Scottish perspective. *Journal of Learning Disabilities*, 28(7), 386–390

Murphy, D. A., Pelham, W. E. and Lang, A. R. (1992) Aggression in boys with attention deficit–hyperactive disorder. *Journal of Abnormal Child Psychology*, 20, 451–466

Musun-Miller, L. (1990) Sociometrics with preschool children: agreement between different strategies. *Journal of Applied Developmental Psychology*, 11, 195–207

Myklebust, H. R. (1975) Non-verbal learning disabilities: assessment and intervention. In H. R. Myklebust (ed.), *Progress in Learning Disabilities: Vol 2*, New York: Grune & Stratton

Nabuzoka, D. (1993) Social Perception, Social Cognition and Behaviour of Children with Learning Disabilities, unpublished PhD thesis, University of Sheffield

Nabuzoka, D. (1999) Can a social cognitive deficit hypothesis explain social adjustment problems of children with learning difficulties? Paper presented at the IXth European Conference on Developmental Psychology. Spetses, Greece, 1–5 September

Nabuzoka, D. and Rønning, J. A. (1997) Social acceptance of children with intellectual disabilities in an integrated school setting in Zambia: a pilot study. *International Journal of Disability, Development and Education*, 44, 105–115

Nabuzoka, D. and Smith, P. K. (1993) Sociometric status and social behaviour of children with and without learning difficulties. *Journal of Child Psychology and Psychiatry*, 34, 1435–1448

Nabuzoka, D. and Smith, P. K. (1995) Identification of expressions of emotions by children with and without learning disabilities. *Learning Disabilities Research and Practice*, 10, 91–101

Nabuzoka, D. and Smith, P. K. (1999) Distinguishing serious and playful fighting by children with learning disabilities and nondisabled children. *Journal of Child Psychology and Psychiatry*, 40, 883–890

Newberry, M. K. and Parish, T. S. (1987) Enhancement of attitudes toward handicapped children through social interactions. *Journal of Social Psychology*, 127, 59–62

Newcomb, A. F. and Bukowski, W. M. (1983) Social impact and social preference as determinants of children's peer group status. *Developmental Psychology*, 19, 856–876

Ochoa, S. H. and Olivarez, A. (1995) A meta-analysis of peer rating sociometric studies of pupils with learning disabilities. *Journal of Special Education*, 29, 1–19

Ochoa, S. H. and Palmer, D. J. (1991) A sociometric analysis of between-group differences and within-group status variability of Hispanic learning-disabled and nonhandicapped pupils in academic and play contexts. *Learning Disability Quarterly*, 14, 208–218

Odom, S. L. and Brown, W. H. (1993) Social interaction skills interventions for young children with disabilities in integrated settings. In C. Peck, S. Odom and D. Bricker (eds), *Integrating Young Children with Disabilities into Community Programs: Ecological Perspectives on Research and Implementation*, Baltimore: Brookes

Odom, S. L., Hoyson, M., Jamieson, B. and Strain, P. S. (1985) Increasing handicapped preschoolers' peer social interactions: cross-setting and component analysis. *Journal of Applied Behaviour Analysis*, 18, 3–17

Odom, S. L. and Strain, P. S. (1984) Peer mediated approaches to promoting children's social interaction: a review. *American Journal of Orthopsychiatry*, 54, 544–557

Oliva, A. H. and LaGreca, A. M. (1988) Children with learning disabilities: social goals and strategies. *Journal of Learning Disabililties*, 21, 301–306

Ollendick, T. H., Greene, R. W., Francis, G. and Baum, C. G. (1991) Sociometric status: its stability and validity among neglected, rejected and popular children. *Journal of Child Psychology and Psychiatry*, 32, 525–534

Olweus, D. (1991) Bully/victim problems among school children: basic facts and effects of a school based intervention program. In D. Pepler and K. Rubin (eds), *The Development and Treatment of Childhood Aggression* (pp. 411–448), Hillsdale, NJ: Lawrence Erlbaum

O'Moore, A. M. and Hillery, B. (1989) Bullying in Dublin schools. *Irish Journal of Psychology*, 10, 426–441

Oster, H. (1981) 'Recognition' of emotional expression in infancy? In M. E. Lamb and L. R. Sherrod (eds), *Infant Social Cognition: Empirical and Theoretical Issues* (pp. 85–125), Hillsdale, NJ: Lawrence Erlbaum

Palmer, D. S., Borthwick-Duffy, S. A. and Widaman, K. (1998) Parent perceptions of inclusive practices for their children with significant cognitive disabilities. *Exceptional Children*, 64, 271–282

Parker, J. G. and Asher, S. (1987) Peer relations and later personal adjustments: are low-accepted children at risk? *Psychological Bulletin*, 102, 357–389

Parkhurst, J. T. and Asher, S. R. (1992) Peer rejection in middle school: subgroup differences in behaviour, loneliness and interpersonal concerns. *Developmental Psychology*, 28, 231–241

Peagam, E. (1994) Special needs or educational apartheid? The emotional and behavioural difficulties of Afro-Caribbean children. *Support for Learning*, 9(1), 33–38

Pearl, R., Donahue, M. and Bryan, T. (1986) Social relationships of learning-disabled children. In J. K. Torgesen and B. Y. L. Wong (eds), *Psychological and Educational Perspectives on Learning Disabilities*, London: Academic Press

Pellegrini, A. D. (1988) Elementary school children's rough-and-tumble play and social competence. *Developmental Psychology*, 24, 802–806

Perlmutter, B. F. (1986) Personality variables and peer relations of children and adolescents with learning disabilities. In S. J. Ceci (ed.), *Handbook of Cognitive, Social and Neuropsychological Aspects of Learning Disabilities: Vol. 1*, London: Lawrence Erlbaum

Perlmutter, B. and Bryan, J. H. (1984) First impressions, ingratiation and the learning disabled child. *Journal of Learning Disabilities*, 17, 157–161

Philippot, P. and Fieldman, R. S. (1990) Age and social competence in preschoolers' decoding of facial expression. *British Journal of Social Psychology*, 29, 43–54

Piaget, J. (1965) *The Moral Judgement of the Child*, New York: Free Press

Piaget, J. (1970) *The Science of Education and Psychology of the Child*, New York: Grossman

Porter, R. H., Ramsey, B., Tremblay, A. and Crawley, S. (1978) Social interactions in heterogeneous groups of retarded and normally developing children: an observational study. In G. P. Sackett (ed.), *Observing Behaviour: Vol. 1. Theory and Applications in Mental Retardation*, Baltimore: University Park Press

Pritchard, D. G. (1963) *Education of the Handicapped, 1760–1960*, London: Routledge & Kegan Paul

Quiggle, N. L., Garber, J., Panak, W. F. and Dodge, K. A. (1992) Social information processing in aggressive and depressed children. *Child Development*, 63, 1305–1320

Reichenbach, L. and Masters, J. C. (1983) Children's use of expressive and contextual cues in judgements of emotion. *Child Development*, 54, 993–1004

Roberts, C., Pratt, C. and Leach, D. (1991) Classroom and playground interaction of students with and without disabilities. *Exceptional Children*, 57, 212–224

Roberts, C. and Zubrick, S. (1993) Factors influencing the social status of children with mild academic disabilities in regular classrooms. *Exceptional Children*, 59, 192–202

Rønning, J. A. and Nabuzoka, D. (1993) Promoting social interaction and status of children with intellectual disabilities in Zambia. *Journal of Special Education*, 27, 277–305

Rothlisberg, B. A., Hill, R. and Damato, R. C. (1994) Social acceptance by their peers of children with mental retardation. *Psychological Reports*, 74, 239–242

Rourke, B. (1989) *Non-verbal Learning Disabilities: The Syndrome and the Model*, New York: Guilford

Rubin, K. H. and Krasnor, L. R. (1986) Social cognitive and social behavioural perspectives on problem solving. In M. Perlmutter (ed.), *Minnesota Symposium on Child Psychology: Vol. 18* (pp. 1–68), Hillsdale, NJ: Lawrence Erlbaum

Rutter, M. and Yule, W. (1977) Reading difficulties. In M. Rutter and L. Hersov (eds), *Child Psychiatry* (pp. 556–575), Oxford: Blackwell

Saarni, C. (1979) Children's understanding of display rules for expressive behaviour. *Developmental Psychology*, 15, 424–429

Sabornie, E. J. (1990) Extended sociometric status of adolescents with mild handicaps: a cross-categorical perspective. *Exceptionality*, 1, 197–209

Sainato, D., Goldstein, H. and Strain, P. (1992) Effects of self-evaluation on pre-school children's use of social interaction strategies with their classmates with autism. *Journal of Applied Behavioual Analysis*, 7, 475–500

Sainato, D. M., Zigmond, N. and Strain, P. (1983) Social status and initiations of interaction by learning disabled students in a regular education setting. *Analysis and Intervention in Developmental Disabilities*, 3, 71–87

Sasso, G. M. and Rude, H. A. (1987) Unprogrammed effects of training high-status peers to interact with severely handicapped children. *Journal of Applied Behavior Analysis*, 20, 35–44

Sater, G. M. and French, D. C. (1989) A comparison of the social competencies of learning-disabled and low-achieving elementary-aged children. *Journal of Special Education*, 23, 29–42

Schaefer, E. S. and Edgerton, M. (1978) *Classroom Behaviour Inventory*, Chapel Hill: University of North Carolina

Schwarzwald, J. and Hoffman, M. A. (1993) Academic status and ethnicity as determinants of social acceptance. *Journal of Cross-Cultural Psychology*, 24, 71–80

Scranton, T. and Ryckman, D. (1979) Sociometric status of learning disabled children in an integrative program. *Journal of Learning Disabilities*, 12, 402–407

Selman, R. L. (1980) *The Growth of Interpersonal Understanding: Developmental and Clinical Analyses*, New York: Academic Press

Selman, R. L. and Byrne, D. F. (1974) A structural–developmental analysis of levels of role taking in middle childhood. *Child Development*, 45, 803–806

Shantz, C. U. (1975) The development of social cognition. In E. M. Hethering-ton (ed.), *Review of Child Development Research: Vol. 5*, Chicago: University of Chicago

Shantz, C. U. (1983) Social cognition. In J. H. Flavell and E. M. Markman (eds), *P. H. Mussen's Handbook of Child Psychology:Vol. 4. Cognitive Development* (pp. 495–555), New York: John Wiley

Sherrod, L. R. (1981) Issues in cognitive–perceptual development: the special case of social stimuli. In M. E. Lamb and L. R. Sherrod (eds), *Infant Social Cognition: Empirical and Theoretical Issues* (pp. 11–36), Hillsdale, NJ: Lawrence Erlbaum

Siperstein, G. N., Budoff, M. and Bak, J. J. (1980) Effects of labels 'mentally retarded' and 'retard' of the social acceptability of mentally retarded children. *American Journal of Mental Deficiency*, 84, 596–601

Siperstein, G. N. and Goding, M. J. (1983) *Social Integration of Learning Disabled Children in Regular Classrooms*, Greenwich, CT: JAI Press

Sisterhen, D. H. and Gerber, P. J. (1989) Auditory, visual and multisensory non-verbal social perception in adolescents with and without learning disabilites. *Journal of Learning Disabilities*, 22, 245–249 and 257

Sloper, T. and Tyler, S. (1992) Integration of children with severe learning difficulties in mainstream schools: evaluation of a pilot study. *Educational and Child Psychology*, 9(4), 34–45

Smith, D. C. (1986) Interpersonal problem-solving skills of retarded and non-retarded children. *Applied Research in Mental Retardation*, 7, 431–442

Smith, P. K. (1991) The silent nightmare: bullying and victimisation in school peer groups. *The Psychologist: Bulletin of the British Psychological Society*, 4, 243–248

Spafford, C. S. and Grosser, G. S. (1993) The social misperception syndrome in children with learning disabilities: social causes versus neurological variables. *Journal of Learning Disabilities*, 26, 178–189 and 198

Speckman, N. (1981) Dyadic verbal communication abilities of learning disabled and normally achieving fourth- and fifth-grade boys. *Learning Disabilities Quarterly*, 4, 139–151

Spence, S. H. (1985) *Social Skills Training with Children and Adolescents: A Counsellor's Manual*, Windsor: NFER–Nelson

Spence, S. H. (1987) The relationship between social–cognitive skills and peer sociometric status. *British Journal of Developmental Psychology*, 5, 347–356

Spence, S. H. (1991) Developments in the assessment of social skills and social competence in children. *Behaviour Change*, 8, 148–166

Sprouse, C. A., Hall, C. W., Webster, R. E. and Bolen, L. M. (1998) Social perception in students with learning disabilities and attention deficit/hyperactivity disorder. *Journal of Non-verbal Behaviour*, 22, 125–134

Stiliadis, K. and Wiener, J. (1989) Relationship between social perception and peer status in children with learning disabilities. *Journal of Learning Disabilities*, 22, 624–629

Stobart, G. (1986) Is integrating the handicapped psychologically defensible? *The Psychologist: Bulletin of the British Psychological Society*, 39, 1–3

Stone, W. L. and LaGreca, A. M. (1990) The social status of children with learning disabilities: a re-examination. *Journal of Learning Disabilities*, 23, 32–37

Strain, P. S. and Odom, S. L. (1986) Effective intervention for social skill development of exceptional children. *Exceptional Children*, 52, 543–551

Strain, P. S. and Shores, R. E. (1977) Social interaction development among behaviorally handicapped preschool children: research and educational implications. *Psychology in the Schools*, 14, 493–502

Strayer, J. (1986) Children's attributions regarding the situational determinants of emotion in self and others. *Developmental Psychology*, 22, 649–654

Sturge, C. (1982) Reading retardation and anti social behaviour. *Journal of Child Psychology and Psychiatry*, 23, 21–31

Sutton, J., Smith, P. K. and Swettenham, J. (1999) Bullying and 'theory of mind': a citique of the 'social skills deficit' view of antisocial behaviour. *Social Development*, 8, 117–127

Swanson, H. L. and Malone, S. (1992) Social skills and learning disabilities: a meta-analysis of the literature. *School Psychology Review*, 21, 427–443

Taylor, A. R. (1990) Behavioral subtypes of low-achieving children: differences in school social adjustment. *Journal of Applied Developmental Psychology*, 11,

487–498

Taylor, A. R., Asher, S. R. and Williams, G. A. (1987) The social adaptation of mainstreamed mildly retarded children. *Child Development*, 58, 1321–1334

Templeman, T. P., Fredericks, H. D. B. and Udell, T. (1989) Integration of children with moderate and severe handicaps into a day care centre. *Journal of Early Intervention*, 13, 315–328

Terry, R. and Coie, J. D. (1991) A comparison of methods for defining sociometric status among children. *Developmental Psychology*, 27, 867–880

Thompson, D. and Arora, T. (1991) Why do children bully? An evaluation of the long-term effectiveness of a whole-school policy to minimise bullying. *Pastoral Care in Education*, 9, 8–12

Thompson, D., Whitney, I. and Smith, P. K. (1994) Bullying of children with special needs in mainstream schools. *Support for Learning*, 9(3), 103–106

Thompson, O. M. (1985) The nonverbal dilemma. *Journal of Learning Disabilities*, 18, 400–402

Toro, P. A., Weissberg, R. P., Guare, J. and Liebenstein, N. L. (1990) A comparison of children with and without learning disabilities on social problem-solving skills, school behavior, and family background. *Journal of Learning Disabilities*, 23, 115–120

Townsend, M. A. R., Wilton, K. M. and Vakilirad, T. (1993) Children's attitudes toward peers with intellectual disability. *Journal of Intellectual Disability Research*, 37, 405–411

Tur-Kaspa, H. and Bryan, T. (1994) Social information processing of students with learning disabilities. *Journal of Learning Disabilities Research and Practice*, 9, 12–23

Tur-Kaspa, H. and Bryan, T. (1995) Teachers' ratings of the social competence and school adjustment of students with LD in elementary and junior high school. *Journal of Learning Disabilities*, 28, 44–52

Tur-Kaspa, H., Margalit, M. and Most, T. (1999) Reciprocal friendship, reciprocal rejection and socio-emotional adjustment: the social experiences of children with learning disorders over a one-year period. *European Journal of Special Needs Education*, 14(1), 37–48

Voeltz, L. (1980) Children's attitudes towards handicapped peers. *American Journal of Mental Deficiency*, 84, 455–464

Voeltz, L. (1982) Effects of structured interactions with severely handicapped peers on children's attitudes. *American Journal of Mental Deficiency*, 86, 380–390

Vogel, S. A. and Forness, S. R. (1992) Social functioning in adults with learning disabilities. *School Psychology Review*, 21, 375–386

Walden, T. A. and Field, T. M. (1990) Preschool children's social competence and production and discrimination of affective expressions. *British Journal of Developmental Psychology*, 8, 65–76

Walker, A. S. (1982) Intermodal perception of expressive behaviours by human infants. *Journal of Experimental Child Psychology*, 33, 514–535

Wallbott, H. G. (1991) The robustness of communication of emotion via facial expression: emotion recognition from photographs with deteriorated pictorial quality. *European Journal of Social Psychology*, 21, 89–98

Warnock, H. M. (1978) *Special Education Needs: Report of the Committee of Enquiry into the Education of Handicapped Children and Young People*, London: HMSO

Weinstein, R. S., Marshall, H. H., Brattesani, K. A. and Middlestadt, S. E. (1982) Student perceptions of differential teacher treatment in open and traditional classrooms. *Journal of Educational Psychology*, 74, 678–692

Weiss, E. (1984) Learning disabled children's understanding of social interactions of peers. *Journal of Learning Disabilities*, 17, 612–615

Wenz-Gross, M. and Siperstein, G. N. (1998) Students with learning problems at risk in middle school: stress, social support, and adjustment. *Exceptional Children*, 65, 91–100

Whitney, I. and Smith, P. K. (1993) A survey of the nature and extent of bullying in junior/middle and secondary schools. *Educational Research*, 35(1), 3–25

Wiener, J. (1980) A theoretical model of the acquisition of peer relationships of learning disabled children. *Journal of Learning Disabilities*, 13, 506–511

Wiggers, M. and van Lieshout, C. F. M. (1985) Development of recognition of emotions: children's reliance on situational and facial expressive cues. *Developmental Psychology*, 21, 338–349

Wiig, E. H. and Harris, S. P. (1974) Perception and interpretation of non-verbal expressed emotions by adolescents with learning disabilities. *Perceptual and Motor Skills*, 38, 239–245

Williams, B. T. R. and Gilmour, J. D. (1994) Annotation: sociometry and peer relationships. *Journal of Child Psychology and Psychiatry*, 35, 997–1013

Wills, T. (1981) Downward comparison principles in social psychology. *Psychological Bulletin*, 106, 231–246

Yeates, K. O. and Selman, R. L. (1989) Social competence in the schools: towards an integrative developmental model for intervention. *Developmental Review*, 9, 64–100

Youniss, J. (1980) *Parents and Peers in Social Development*, Chicago: University of Chicago Press

Zahn-Waxler, C., Radke-Yarrow, M. and Brady-Smith, J. (1977) Social perspective-taking and prosocial behaviour. *Developmental Psychology*, 13, 87–88

Zigler, E. and Hall, N. (1986) Mainstreaming and the philosophy of normalization. In C. J. Meisel (ed.) *Mainstreaming Handicapped Children: Outcomes, Controversies, and New Directions*, London: Education Authority

Subject index

Bold type refers to **figures**. Page numbers in *italic* type refer to *tables*.

Author index

Donation